He Taught Love

Jesus' Lessons for Living

E. G. White

Review and Herald® Publishing Association
Hagerstown, MD 21740

This book was
Designed by Byron Steele
All photographs supplied by PhotoDisc
Type set: 11/14 Goudy

PRINTED IN U.S.A.

ISBN 0-8280-1274-1 HHES
ISBN 0-8280-1360-8 FHES

ASI Student Project

"All these things spake Jesus unto the multitude in parables" (Matt. 13:34).

Stories With a Point

In Christ's parable teaching the same principle is seen as in His own mission to the world. That we might become acquainted with His divine character and life, Christ took our nature and dwelt among us. Divinity was revealed in humanity, the invisible glory in the visible human form. Men could learn of the unknown through the known; heavenly things were revealed through the earthly; God was made manifest in the likeness of men. So it was in Christ's teaching: the unknown was illustrated by the known; divine truths, by earthly things with which the people were most familiar.

The Scripture says, "All these things spake Jesus unto the multitude in parables; . . . that it might be fulfilled which was spoken by the prophet, saying, I will open My mouth in parables; I will utter things which have been kept secret from the foundation of the world." Matthew 13:34, 35. Natural things were the medium for the spiritual; the things of nature and the life-experience of His hearers were connected with the truths of the written word. Leading thus from the natural to the spiritual kingdom, Christ's parables are links in the chain of truth that unites man with God, and earth with heaven.

In His teaching from nature Christ was speaking of the things which His own hands had made, and which had qualities and powers that He Himself had imparted. In their original perfection all created things were an expression of the thought of God. To Adam and Eve in their Eden home nature was full of the knowledge of God, teeming with divine instruction. Wisdom spoke to the eye and was received into the heart, for they communed with God in His created works. As soon as the holy pair transgressed the law of the Most High, the brightness from the face of God departed from the face of nature. The earth is now marred and defiled by sin. Yet even in its blighted state much that is beautiful remains. God's object lessons are not obliterated; rightly understood, nature speaks of her Creator.

In the days of Christ these lessons had been lost sight of. Men had well-nigh ceased to discern God in His works. The sinfulness of humanity had cast a pall over the fair face of creation; and instead of manifesting God, His works became a barrier that concealed Him. Men "worshipped and served the creature more than the Creator." Thus the heathen "became vain in their imaginations, and their foolish heart was darkened." Romans 1:25, 21. So in Israel man's teaching had been put in the place of God's. Not only the things of nature but the sacrificial service and the Scriptures themselves—all given to reveal God—were so perverted that they became the means of concealing Him.

The scenes upon which the eye daily rests were all connected with some spiritual truth.

Christ sought to remove that which obscured the truth. The veil that sin has cast over the face of nature He came to draw aside, bringing to view the spiritual glory that all things were created to reflect. His words placed the teachings of nature as well as of the Bible in a new aspect and made them a new revelation.

Jesus plucked the beautiful lily, and placed it in the hands of children and youth; and as they looked into His own youthful face, fresh with the sunlight of His Father's countenance, He gave the lesson, "Consider the lilies of the field, how they grow [in the simplicity of natural beauty]; they toil not, neither do they spin: and yet I say unto you, That even Solomon in all his glory was not arrayed like one of these." Then followed the sweet assurance and the important lesson, "Wherefore, if God so clothe the grass of the field, which to day is, and to morrow is cast into the oven, shall He not much more clothe you, O ye of little faith?" Matthew 6:28-30.

In the Sermon on the Mount these words were spoken to others besides children and youth. They were spoken to the multitude, among whom were men and women full of worries and perplexities, and sore with disappointment and sorrow. Jesus continued: "Therefore take no thought, saying, What shall we eat? or, What shall we drink? or, Wherewithal shall we be clothed? (for after all these things do the Gentiles seek:) for your heavenly Father knoweth that ye have need of all these things." Then spreading out His hands to the surrounding multitude, He said, "But seek ye first the kingdom of God, and His righteousness; and all these things shall be added unto you." Verses 31-33.

Thus Christ interpreted the message which He Himself had given to the lilies and the grass of the field. He desires us to read it in every lily and every spire of grass. His words are full of assurance and tend to confirm trust in God.

So wide was Christ's view of truth, so extended His teaching, that every phase of nature was employed in illustrating truth. The scenes upon which the eye daily rests were all connected with some spiritual truth, so that nature is clothed with the parables of the Master.

In the earlier part of His ministry Christ had spoken to the people in words so plain that all His hearers might have grasped truths which would have made them wise unto salvation. But in many hearts the truth had taken no root, and it had been quickly caught away. "Therefore speak I to them in parables," He said: "because they seeing see not; and hearing they hear not, neither do they understand. . . . For this people's heart is waxed gross, and their ears are dull of hearing, and their eyes they have closed." Matthew 13:13-15.

Jesus desired to awaken inquiry. He sought to arouse the careless, and impress truth upon the heart. Parable teaching was popular, and commanded the respect and attention, not only of the Jews, but of the people of other nations. No more effective method of instruction could He have employed. If His hearers had desired a knowledge of divine things, they might have understood His words, for He was always willing to explain them to the honest inquirer.

Again, Christ had truths to present which the people were unprepared to accept or even to understand. For this reason also He taught them in parables. By connecting His teaching with the scenes of life, experience, or nature, He secured their attention and impressed their hearts. Afterward, as they looked upon the objects that illustrated His lessons, they recalled the words of the divine Teacher. To minds that were open to the Holy Spirit the significance of the Saviour's teaching unfolded more and more. Mysteries grew clear, and that which had been hard to grasp became evident.

Jesus sought an avenue to every heart. By using a variety of illustrations He not only presented truth in its different phases but appealed to the different hearers. Their interest was aroused by figures drawn from the surroundings of their daily life. None who listened to the Saviour could feel that they were neglected or forgotten. The humblest, the most sinful, heard in His teaching a voice that spoke to them in sympathy and tenderness.

And He had another reason for teaching in parables. Among the multitudes that gathered about Him there were priests and rabbis, scribes and elders, Herodians and rulers, world-loving, bigoted, ambitious men, who desired above all things to find some accusation against Him. Their spies followed His steps day after day, to catch from His lips something that would cause His condemnation and forever silence the One who seemed to draw the world after Him. The Saviour understood the character of these men, and He presented truth in such a way that they could find nothing by which to bring His case before the Sanhedrin. In parables He rebuked the hypocrisy and wicked works of those who occupied high positions, and in figurative language clothed truth of so cutting a character that had it been spoken in direct denunciation, they would not have listened to His words, and would speedily have put an end to His ministry.

None who listened to the Saviour could feel that they were neglected or forgotten.

But while He evaded the spies, He made truth so clear that error was manifested, and the honest in heart were profited by His lessons. Divine wisdom, infinite grace, were made plain by the things of God's creation. Through nature and the experiences of life men were taught of God. "The invisible things of Him since the creation of the world," were "perceived through the things that are made, even His everlasting power and divinity." Romans 1:20, R.V.

In the Saviour's parable teaching is an indication of what constitutes the true "higher education." Christ might have opened to men the deepest truths of science. He might have unlocked mysteries which have required many centuries of toil and study to penetrate. He might have made suggestions in scientific lines that would have afforded food for thought and stimulus for invention to the close of time. But He did not do this. He said nothing to gratify curiosity or to satisfy man's ambition by opening doors to worldly greatness. In all His teaching Christ brought the mind of man in contact with the Infinite Mind. He did not direct the people to study men's theories about God, His word, or His works. He taught them to behold Him as manifested in His works, in His word, and by His providences.

Christ did not deal in abstract theories, but in that which is essential to the development of character, that which will enlarge man's capacity for knowing God, and increase his efficiency to do good. He spoke to men of those truths that relate to the conduct of life and that take hold upon eternity.

In all His teaching Christ brought the mind of man in contact with the Infinite Mind.

It was Christ who directed the education of Israel. Concerning the commandments and ordinances of the Lord He said, "Thou shalt teach them diligently unto thy children, and shalt talk of them when thou sittest in thine house, and when thou walkest by the way, and when thou liest down, and when thou risest up. And thou shalt bind them for a sign upon thine hand, and they shall be as frontlets between thine eyes. And thou shalt write them upon the posts of thy house, and on thy gates." Deuteronomy 6:7-9. In His own teaching Jesus showed how this command is to be fulfilled—how the laws and principles of God's kingdom can be so presented as to reveal their beauty and preciousness. When the Lord was training Israel to be the special representatives of Himself, He gave them homes among the hills and valleys. In their home life and their religious service they were brought in constant contact with nature and with the word of God. So Christ taught His disciples by the lake, on the mountainside, in the fields and groves, where they could look upon the things of nature by which He illustrated His teachings. And as they learned of Christ they put their knowledge to use by cooperating with Him in His work.

So through the creation we are to become acquainted with the Creator. The book of nature is a great lesson book, which in connection with the Scriptures we are to use in teaching others of His character and guiding lost sheep back to the fold of God. As the works of God are studied the Holy Spirit flashes conviction into the mind. It is not the conviction that logical reasoning produces; but unless the mind has become too dark to know God, the eye too dim to see Him, the ear too dull to hear His voice, a deeper meaning is grasped, and the sublime, spiritual truths of the written word are impressed on the heart.

In these lessons direct from nature there is a simplicity and purity that makes them of the highest value. All need the teaching to be derived from this source. In itself the beauty of nature leads the soul away from sin and worldly attractions, and toward purity, peace, and God. Too often the minds of students are occupied with men's theories and speculations, falsely called science and philosophy. They need to be brought into close contact with nature. Let them learn that creation and Christianity have one God. Let them be taught to see the harmony of the natural with the spiritual. Let everything which their eyes see or their hands handle be made a lesson in character building. Thus the mental powers will be strengthened, the character developed, the whole life ennobled.

Christ's purpose in parable teaching was in direct line with the purpose of the Sabbath. God gave to men the memorial of His creative power, that they might discern Him in the works of His hand. The Sabbath bids us behold in His created works the glory of the Creator. And it was because He desired us to do this that Jesus bound up His precious lessons with the beauty of natural things. On the holy rest day, above all other days, we should study the messages that God has written for us in nature. We should study the Saviour's parables where He spoke them, in the fields and groves, under the open sky, among the grass and flowers. As we come close to the heart of nature Christ makes His presence real to us, and speaks to our hearts of His peace and love.

And Christ has linked His teaching, not only with the day of rest, but with the week of toil. He has wisdom for him who drives the plow and sows the seed. In the plowing and sowing, the tilling and reaping, He teaches us to see an illustration of His work of grace in the heart. So in every line of useful labor and every association of life, He desires us to find a lesson of divine truth. Then our daily toil will no longer absorb our attention and lead us to forget God; it will continually remind us of our Creator and Redeemer. The thought of God will run like a thread of gold through all our homely cares and occupations. For us the glory of His face will again rest upon the face of nature. We shall ever be learning new lessons of heavenly truth, and growing into the image of His purity. Thus shall we "be taught of the Lord"; and in the lot wherein we are called, we shall "abide with God." Isaiah 54:13; 1 Corinthians 7:24.

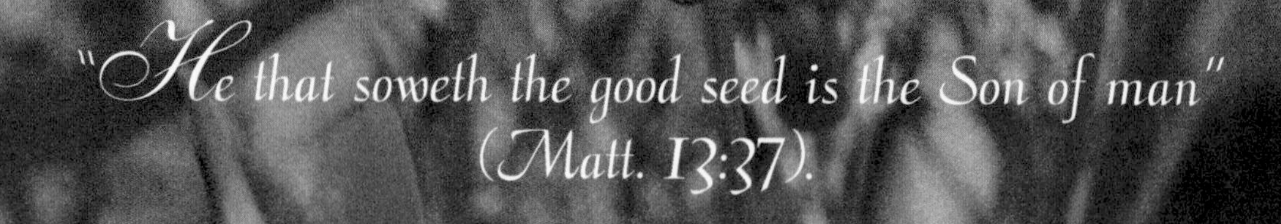
"He that soweth the good seed is the Son of man"
(Matt. 13:37).

Based on Matthew 13:1-9, 18-23; Mark 4:1-20; Luke 8:4-15

SOWING THE GOOD SEED

By the parable of the sower Christ illustrates the things of the kingdom of heaven and the work of the great Husbandman for His people. Like a sower in the field, He came to scatter the heavenly grain of truth. And His parable teaching itself was the seed with which the most precious truths of His grace were sown. Because of its simplicity the parable of the sower has not been valued as it should be. From the naturel seed cast into the soil, Christ desires to lead our minds to the gospel seed, the sowing of which results in bringing man back to his loyalty to God. He who gave the parable of the tiny seed is the Sovereign of heaven, and the same laws that govern earthly seed sowing govern the sowing of the seeds of truth.

By the Sea of Galilee a company had gathered to see and hear Jesus—an eager, expectant throng. The sick were there, lying on their mats, waiting to present their cases before Him. It was Christ's God-given right to heal the woes of a sinful race, and He now rebuked disease and diffused around Him life and health and peace.

As the crowd continued to increase, the people pressed close about Christ until there was no room to receive them. Then, speaking a word to the men in their fishing boats, He stepped into the boat that was waiting to take Him across the lake, and bidding His disciples push off a little from the land, He spoke to the multitude upon the shore.

Beside the sea lay the beautiful plain of Gennesaret, beyond rose the hills, and upon hillside and plain both sowers and reapers were busy, the one casting seed and the other harvesting the early grain. Looking upon the scene, Christ said—

"Behold, the sower went forth to sow; and as he sowed, some seeds fell by the way side, and the birds came and devoured them" (R.V.); "some fell upon stony places, where they had not much earth: and forthwith they sprung up, because they had no deepness of earth: and when the sun was up, they were scorched; and because they had no root, they withered away. And some fell among thorns; and the thorns sprung up, and choked them: but other fell into good ground, and brought forth fruit, some an hundredfold, some sixtyfold, some thirtyfold."

Christ's mission was not understood by the people of His time. The manner of His coming was not in accordance with their expectations. The Lord Jesus was the foundation of the whole Jewish economy. Its imposing services were of divine appointment. They were designed to teach the people that at the time appointed One would come to whom those ceremonies pointed. But the Jews had exalted the forms and ceremonies, and had lost sight of their object. The traditions, maxims, and enactments of men hid from them the lessons which God intended to convey. These maxims and traditions became an obstacle to their understanding and practice of true religion. And when the Reality came, in the person of Christ, they did not recognize in Him the fulfillment of all their types, the substance of all their shadows. They rejected the antitype, and clung to their types and useless ceremonies. The Son of God had come, but they continued to ask for a sign. The message, "Repent ye: for the kingdom of heaven is at hand," they answered by demands for a miracle. (Matthew 3:2.) The gospel of Christ was a stumbling block to them because they demanded signs instead of a Saviour. They expected the Messiah to prove His claims by mighty deeds of conquest, to establish His empire on the ruins of earthly kingdoms. This expectation Christ answered in the parable of the sower. Not by force of arms, not by violent interpositions, was the kingdom of God to prevail, but by the implanting of a new principle in the hearts of men.

The gospel of Christ was a stumbling block to them because they demanded signs instead of a Saviour.

"He that soweth the good seed is the Son of man." Matthew 13:37. Christ had come, not as a king, but as a sower; not for the overthrow of kingdoms, but for the scattering of seed; not to point His followers to earthly triumphs and national greatness, but to a harvest to be gathered after patient toil and through losses and disappointments.

The Pharisees perceived the meaning of Christ's parable, but to them its lesson was unwelcome. They affected not to understand it. To the multitude it involved in still greater mystery the purpose of the new teacher, whose words had so strangely moved their hearts and so bitterly disappointed their ambitions. The disciples themselves had not understood the parable, but their interest was awakened. They came to Jesus privately and asked for an explanation.

This was the desire which Christ wished to arouse, that He might give them more definite instruction. He explained the parable to them, as He will make plain His word to all who seek Him in sincerity of heart. Those who study the word of God with hearts open to the enlightenment of the Holy Spirit, will not remain in darkness as to the meaning of the word. "If any man willeth to do His will," Christ said, "he shall know of the teaching, whether it be of God, or whether I speak from Myself." John 7:17, R.V. All who come to Christ for a clearer knowledge of the truth will receive it. He will unfold to them the mysteries of the kingdom of heaven, and these mysteries will be understood by the heart that longs to know the truth. A heavenly light will shine into the soul temple, and will be revealed to others as the bright shining of a lamp on a dark path.

"The sower went forth to sow." R.V. In the East the state of affairs was so unsettled, and there was so great danger from violence that the people dwelt chiefly in walled towns, and the husbandmen went forth daily to their labor outside the walls. So Christ, the heavenly Sower, went forth to sow. He left His home of security and peace, left the glory that He had with the Father before the world was, left His position upon the throne of the universe. He went forth, a suffering, tempted man; went forth in solitude, to sow in tears, to water with His blood, the seed of life for a world lost.

His servants in like manner must go forth to sow. When called to become a sower of the seed of truth Abraham was bidden, "Get thee out of thy country, and from thy kindred, and from thy father's house, unto a land that I will shew thee." Genesis 12:1. "And he went out, not knowing whither he went." Hebrews 11:8. So to the apostle Paul, praying in the temple at Jerusalem, came the message from God, "Depart: for I will send thee far hence unto the Gentiles." Acts 22:21. So those who are called to unite with Christ must leave all, in order to follow Him. Old associations must be broken up, plans of life relinquished, earthly hopes surrendered. In toil and tears, in solitude, and through sacrifice, must the seed be sown."

"The sower soweth the word." Christ came to sow the world with truth. Ever since the fall of man Satan has been sowing the seeds of error. It was by a lie that he first gained control over man, and thus he still works to overthrow God's kingdom in the earth and to bring men under his power. A sower from a higher world, Christ came to sow the seeds of truth. He who had stood in the councils of God, who had dwelt in the innermost sanctuary of the Eternal, could bring to men the pure principles of truth. Ever since the fall of man Christ had been the Revealer of truth to the world. By Him the incorruptible seed, "the word of God, which liveth and abideth for ever," is communicated to men. (1 Peter 1:23.) In that first promise spoken to our fallen race in Eden, Christ was sowing the gospel seed. But it is to His personal ministry among men and to the work which He thus established that the parable of the sower especially applies.

So Christ . . . went forth in solitude, to sow in tears, to water with His blood, the seed of life for a world lost.

The word of God is the seed. Every seed has in itself a germinating principle. In it the life of the plant is enfolded. So there is life in God's word. Christ says, "The words that I speak unto you, they are spirit, and they are life." John 6:63. "He that heareth My word, and believeth on Him that sent Me, hath everlasting life." John 5:24. In every command and in every promise of the word of God is the power, the very life of God, by which the command may be fulfilled and the promise realized. He who by faith receives the word is receiving the very life and character of God.

Every seed brings forth fruit after its kind. Sow the seed under right conditions, and it will develop its own life in the plant. Receive into the soul by faith the incorruptible seed of the word, and it will bring forth a character and a life after the similitude of the character and the life of God.

The teachers of Israel were not sowing the seed of the word of God. Christ's work as a teacher of truth was in marked contrast to that of the rabbis of His time. They dwelt upon traditions, upon human theories and speculations. Often that which man had taught and written about the word, they put in place of the word itself. Their teaching had no power to quicken the soul. The subject of Christ's teaching and preaching was the word of God. He met questioners with a plain, "It is written." "What saith the Scriptures?" "How readest thou?" At every opportunity, when an interest was awakened by either friend or foe, He sowed the seed of the word. He who is the Way, the Truth, and the Life, Himself the living Word, points to the Scriptures, saying, "They are they which testify of Me." And "beginning at Moses and all the prophets," He opened to His disciples "in all the scriptures the things concerning Himself." John 5:39; Luke 24:27.

He who by faith receives the word is receiving the very life and character of God.

Christ's servants are to do the same work. In our day, as of old, the vital truths of God's word are set aside for human theories and speculations. Many professed ministers of the gospel do not accept the whole Bible as the inspired word. One wise man rejects one portion; another questions another part. They set up their judgment as superior to the word; and the Scripture which they do teach rests upon their own authority. Its divine authenticity is destroyed. Thus the seeds of infidelity are sown broadcast, for the people become confused and know not what to believe. There are many beliefs that the mind has no right to entertain. In the days of Christ the rabbis put a forced, mystical construction upon many portions of Scripture. Because the plain teaching of God's word condemned their practices, they tried to destroy its force. The same thing is done today. The word of God is made to appear mysterious and obscure in order to excuse transgression of His law. Christ rebuked these practices in His day. He taught that the word of God was to be understood by all. He pointed to the Scriptures as of unquestionable authority, and we should do the same. The Bible is to be presented as the word of the infinite God, as the end of all controversy and the foundation of all faith.

The Bible has been robbed of its power, and the results are seen in a lowering of the tone of spiritual life. In the sermons from many pulpits of today there is not that divine manifestation which awakens the conscience and brings life to the soul. The hearers cannot say, "Did not our heart burn within us, while He talked with us by the way, and while He opened to us the scriptures?" Luke 24:32. There are many who are crying out for the living God, longing for the divine presence. Philosophical theories or literary essays, however brilliant, cannot satisfy the heart. The assertions and inventions of men are of no value. Let the word of God speak to the people. Let those who have heard only traditions and human theories and maxims hear the voice of Him whose word can renew the soul unto everlasting life.

Christ's favorite theme was the paternal tenderness and abundant grace of God; He dwelt much upon the holiness of His character and His law; He presented Himself to the people as the way, the truth, and the life. Let these be the themes of Christ's ministers. Present the truth as it is in Jesus. Make plain the requirements of the law and the gospel. Tell the people of Christ's life of self-denial and sacrifice; of His humiliation and death; of His resurrection and ascension; of His intercession for them in the courts of God; of His promise, "I will come again, and receive you unto Myself." John 14:3.

Instead of discussing erroneous theories, or seeking to combat the opponents of the gospel, follow the example of Christ. Let fresh truths from God's treasure house flash into life. "Preach the word." "Sow beside all waters." "Be instant in season, out of season." "He that hath My word, let him speak My word faithfully. What is the chaff to the wheat? saith the Lord." "Every word of God is pure. . . . Add thou not unto His words, lest He reprove thee, and thou be found a liar." 2 Timothy 4:2; Isaiah 32:20; Jeremiah 23:28; Proverbs 30:5, 6.

"The sower soweth the word." Here is presented the great principle which should underlie all educational work. "The seed is the word of God." But in too many schools of our day God's word is set aside. Other subjects occupy the mind. The study of infidel authors holds a large place in the educational system. Skeptical sentiments are interwoven in the matter placed in school books. Scientific research becomes misleading, because its discoveries are misinterpreted and perverted. The word of God is compared with the supposed teachings of science, and is made to appear uncertain and untrustworthy. Thus the seeds of doubt are planted in the minds of the youth, and in time of temptation they spring up. When faith in God's word is lost, the soul has no guide, no safeguard. The youth are drawn into paths which lead away from God and from everlasting life.

To this cause may in great degree be attributed the widespread iniquity in our world today. When the word of God is set aside, its power to restrain the evil passions of the natural heart is rejected. Men sow to the flesh, and of the flesh they reap corruption.

And here, too, is the great cause of mental weakness and inefficiency. In turning from God's word to feed on the writings of uninspired men, the mind becomes dwarfed and cheapened. It is not brought in contact with deep, broad principles of eternal truth. The understanding adapts itself to the comprehension of the things with which it is familiar, and in this devotion to finite things it is weakened, its power is contracted, and after a time it becomes unable to expand.

Present the truth as it is in Jesus. Make plain the requirements of the law and the gospel.

All this is false education. The work of every teacher should be to fasten the mind of the youth upon the grand truths of the word of inspiration. This is the education essential for this life and for the life to come.

And let it not be thought that this will prevent

the study of the sciences, or cause a lower standard in education. The knowledge of God is as high as heaven and as broad as the universe. There is nothing so ennobling and invigorating as a study of the great themes which concern our eternal life. Let the youth seek to grasp these God-given truths, and their minds will expand and grow strong in the effort. It will bring every student who is a doer of the word into a broader field of thought, and secure for him a wealth of knowledge that is imperishable.

The education to be secured by searching the Scriptures is an experimental knowledge of the plan of salvation. Such an education will restore the image of God in the soul. It will strengthen and fortify the mind against temptation, and fit the learner to become a co-worker with Christ in His mission of mercy to the world. It will make him a member of the heavenly family, and prepare him to share the inheritance of the saints in light.

Christ taught the truth because He was the truth.

But the teacher of sacred truth can impart only that which he himself knows by experience. "The sower sowed *his* seed." Christ taught the truth because He was the truth. His own thought, His character, His life-experience, were embodied in His teaching. So with His servants: those who would teach the word are to make it their own by a personal experience. They must know what it is to have Christ made unto them wisdom and righteousness and sanctification and redemption. In presenting the word of God to others, they are not to make it a suppose-so or a may-be. They should declare with the apostle Peter, "We have not followed cunningly devised fables, when we made known unto you the power and coming of our Lord Jesus Christ, but were eyewitnesses of His majesty." 2 Peter 1:16. Every minister of Christ and every teacher should be able to say with the beloved John, "The life was manifested, and we have seen it, and bear witness, and shew unto you that eternal life, which was with the Father, and was manifested unto us." 1 John 1:2.

The Soil—by the Wayside

That with which the parable of the sower chiefly deals is the effect produced on the growth of the seed by the soil into which it is cast. By this parable Christ was virtually saying to His hearers, It is not safe for you to stand as critics of My work, or to indulge disappointment because it does not meet your ideas. The question of greatest importance to you is, How do you treat My message? Upon your reception or rejection of it your eternal destiny depends.

Explaining the seed that fell by the wayside, He said, "When any one heareth the word of the kingdom, and understandeth it not, then cometh the wicked one, and catcheth away that which was sown in his heart. This is he which received seed by the way side."

The seed sown by the wayside represents the word of God as it falls upon the heart of an inattentive hearer. Like the hard-beaten path, trodden down by the feet of men and beasts, is the heart that becomes a highway for the world's traffic, its pleasures and sins. Absorbed in selfish aims and sinful indulgences, the soul is "hardened through the deceitfulness of sin." Hebrews 3:13. The spiritual faculties are paralyzed. Men hear the word but understand it not. They do not discern that it applies to themselves. They do not realize their need or their danger. They do not perceive the love of Christ, and they pass by the message of His grace as something that does not concern them.

As the birds are ready to catch up the seed from the wayside, so Satan is ready to catch away the seeds of divine truth from the soul. He fears that the word of God may awaken the careless, and take effect upon the hardened heart. Satan and his angels are in the assemblies where the gospel is preached. While angels of heaven endeavor to impress hearts with the word of God, the enemy is on the alert to make the word of no effect. With an earnestness equaled only by his malice, he tries to thwart the work of the Spirit of God. While Christ is drawing the soul by His love, Satan tries to turn away the attention of the one who is moved to seek the Saviour. He engages the mind with worldly schemes. He excites criticism, or insinuates doubt and unbelief. The speaker's choice of language or his manner may not please the hearers, and they dwell upon these defects. Thus the truth they need, and which God has graciously sent them, makes no lasting impression.

Satan has many helpers. Many who profess to be Christians are aiding the tempter to catch away the seeds of truth from other hearts. Many who listen to the preaching of the word of God make it the subject of criticism at home. They sit in judgment on the sermon as they would on the words of a lecturer or a political speaker. The message that should be regarded as the word of the Lord to them is dwelt upon with trifling or sarcastic comment. The minister's character, motives, and actions, and the conduct of fellow members of the church, are freely discussed. Severe judgment is pronounced, gossip or slander repeated, and this in the hearing of the unconverted. Often these things are spoken by parents in the hearing of their own children. Thus are destroyed respect for God's messengers, and reverence for their message. And many are taught to regard lightly God's word itself.

Thus in the homes of professed Christians many youth are educated to be infidels. And the parents question why their children are so little interested in the gospel, and so ready to doubt the truth of the Bible. They wonder that it is so difficult to reach them with moral and religious influences. They do not see that their own example has hardened the hearts of their children. The good seed finds no place to take root, and Satan catches it away.

Men hear the word but understand it not. They do not discern that it applies to themselves.

In Stony Places

"He that received the seed into stony places, the same is he that heareth the word, and anon with joy receiveth it; yet hath he not root in himself, but dureth for a while: for when tribulation or persecution ariseth because of the word, by and by he is offended."

The seed sown upon stony ground finds little depth of soil. The plant springs up quickly, but the root cannot penetrate the rock to find nutriment to sustain its growth, and it soon perishes. Many who make a profession of religion are stony-ground hearers. Like the rock underlying the layer of earth, the selfishness of the natural heart underlies the soil of their good desires and aspirations. The love of self is not subdued. They have not seen the exceeding sinfulness of sin, and the heart has not been humbled under a sense of its guilt. This class may be easily convinced, and appear to be bright converts, but they have only a superficial religion.

It is not because men receive the word immediately, nor because they rejoice in it, that they fall away. As soon as Matthew heard the Saviour's call, immediately he rose up, left all, and followed Him. As soon as the divine word comes to our hearts, God desires us to receive it; and it is right to accept it with joy. "Joy shall be in heaven over one sinner that repenteth." Luke 15:7. And there is joy in the soul that believes on Christ.

It is by the invisible union of the soul with Christ, through faith, that the spiritual life is nourished.

But those who in the parable are said to receive the word immediately, do not count the cost. They do not consider what the word of God requires of them. They do not bring it face to face with all their habits of life, and yield themselves fully to its control.

The roots of the plant strike down deep into the soil, and hidden from sight nourish the life of the plant. So with the Christian; it is by the invisible union of the soul with Christ, through faith, that the spiritual life is nourished. But the stony-ground hearers depend upon self instead of Christ. They trust in their good works and good impulses, and are strong in their own righteousness. They are not strong in the Lord, and in the power of His might. Such a one "hath not root in himself," for he is not connected with Christ.

The hot summer sun, that strengthens and ripens the hardy grain, destroys that which has no depth of root. So he who "hath not root in himself" "dureth for a while:"; but "when tribulation or persecution ariseth because of the word, by and by he is offended." Many receive the gospel as a way of escape from suffering, rather than as a deliverance for sin. They rejoice for a season, for they think that religion will free them from difficulty and trial. While life moves smoothly with them, they may appear to be consistent Christians. But they faint beneath the fiery test of temptation. They cannot bear reproach for Christ's sake. When the word of God points out some cherished sin, or requires self-denial or sacrifice, they are offended. It would cost them too much effort to make a radical change in their life. They look at the present inconvenience and trial, and forget the eternal realities. Like the disciples who left Jesus, they are ready to say, "This is an hard saying; who can hear it?" John 6:60.

There are very many who claim to serve God, but who have no experimental knowledge of Him. Their desire to do His will is based upon their own inclination, not upon the deep conviction of the Holy Spirit. Their conduct is not brought into harmony with the law of God. They profess to accept Christ as their Saviour, but they do not believe that He will give them power to overcome their sins. They have not a personal relation with a living Saviour, and their characters reveal defects both hereditary and cultivated.

It is one thing to assent in a general way to the agency of the Holy Spirit, and another thing to accept His work as a reprover calling to repentance. Many feel a sense of estrangement from God, a realization of their bondage to self and sin; they make efforts for reform, but they do not crucify self. They do not give themselves entirely into the hands of Christ, seeking for divine power to do His will. They are not willing to be molded after the divine similitude. In a general way they acknowledge their imperfections, but they do not give up their particular sins. With each wrong act the old selfish nature is gaining strength.

The only hope for these souls is to realize in themselves the truth of Christ's words to Nicodemus, "Ye must be born again." "Except a man be born again ["from above," margin], he cannot see the kingdom of God." John 3:7, 3.

True holiness is wholeness in the service of God. This is the condition of true Christian living. Christ asks for an unreserved consecration, for undivided service. He demands the heart, the mind, the soul, the strength. Self is not to be cherished. He who lives to himself is not a Christian.

Love must be the principle of action. Love is the underlying principle of God's government in heaven and earth, and it must be the foundation of the Christian's character. This alone can make and keep him steadfast. This alone can enable him to withstand trial and temptation.

And love will be revealed in sacrifice. The plan of redemption was laid in sacrifice—a sacrifice so broad and deep and high that it is immeasurable. Christ gave all for us, and those who receive Christ will be ready to sacrifice all for the sake of their Redeemer. The thought of His honor and glory will come before anything else.

If we love Jesus, we shall love to live for Him, to present our thank offerings to Him, to labor for Him. The very labor will be light. For His sake we shall covet pain and toil and sacrifice. We shall sympathize with His longing for the salvation of men. We shall feel the same tender craving for souls that He has felt.

This is the religion of Christ. Anything short of it is a deception. No mere theory of truth or profession of discipleship will save any soul. We do not belong to Christ unless we are His wholly. It is by halfheartedness in the Christian life that men become feeble in purpose and changeable in desire. The effort to serve both self and Christ makes one a stony-ground hearer, and he will not endure when the test comes upon him.

If we love Jesus, we shall love to live for Him, . . . to labor for Him.

Among Thorns

"He also that received seed among the thorns is he that heareth the word; and the care of this world, and the deceitfulness of riches, choke the word, and he becometh unfruitful."

The gospel seed often falls among thorns and noxious weeds; and if there is not a moral transformation in the human heart, if old habits and practices and the former life of sin are not left behind, if the attributes of Satan are not expelled from the soul, the wheat crop will be choked. The thorns will come to be the crop, and will kill out the wheat.

Grace can thrive only in the heart that is being constantly prepared for the precious seeds of truth. The thorns of sin will grow in any soil; they need no cultivation; but grace must be carefully cultivated. The briers and thorns are always ready to spring up, and the work of purification must advance continually. If the heart is not kept under the control of God, if the Holy Spirit does not work unceasingly to refine and ennoble the character, the old habits will reveal themselves in the life. Men may profess to believe the gospel, but unless they are sanctified by the gospel their profession is of no avail. If they do not gain the victory over sin, then sin is gaining the victory over them. The thorns that have been cut off but not uprooted grow apace, until the soul is overspread with them.

If the heart is not kept under the control of God, . . . old habits will reveal themselves in the life.

Christ specified the things that are dangerous to the soul. As recorded by Mark He mentions the cares of this world, the deceitfulness of riches, and the lusts of other things. Luke specifies the cares, riches, and pleasures of this life. These are what choke the word, the growing spiritual seed. The soul ceases to draw nourishment from Christ, and spirituality dies out of the heart.

"The care of this world." No class is free from the temptation to worldly care. To the poor, toil and deprivation and the fear of want bring perplexities and burdens. To the rich come fear of loss and a multitude of anxious cares. Many of Christ's followers forget the lesson He has bidden us learn from the flowers of the field. They do not trust to His constant care. Christ cannot carry their burden, because they do not cast it upon Him. Therefore the cares of life, which should drive them to the Saviour for help and comfort, separate them from Him.

Many who might be fruitful in God's service become bent on acquiring wealth. Their whole energy is absorbed in business enterprises, and they feel obliged to neglect things of a spiritual nature. Thus they separate themselves from God. We are enjoined in the Scriptures to be "not slothful in business." Romans 12:11. We are to labor that we may impart to him who needs. Christians must work, they must engage in business, and they can do this without committing sin. But many become so absorbed in business that they have no time for prayer, no time for the study of the Bible, no time to seek and serve God. At times the longings of the soul go out for holiness and heaven, but there is no time to turn aside from the din of the world to listen to the majestic and authoritative utterances of the Spirit of God. The things of eternity are made subordinate; the things of the world supreme. It is impossible for seed of the word to bring forth fruit, for the life of the soul is given to nourish the thorns of worldliness.

And many who are working with a very different purpose, fall into a like error. They are working for others' good; their duties are pressing, their responsibilities are many, and they allow their labor to crowd out devotion. Communion with God through prayer and a study of His word is neglected. They forget that Christ has said, "Without Me ye can do nothing." John 15:5. They walk apart from Christ, their life is not pervaded by His grace, and the characteristics of self are revealed. Their service is marred by desire for supremacy, and the harsh, unlovely traits of the unsubdued heart. Here is one of the chief secrets of failure in Christian work. This is why its results are often so meager.

"The deceitfulness of riches." The love of riches has an infatuating, deceptive power. Too often those who possess worldly treasure forget that it is God who gives them power to get wealth. They say, "My power and the might of mine hand hath gotten me this wealth." Deuteronomy 8:17. Their riches, instead of awakening gratitude to God, lead to the exaltation of self. They lose the sense of their dependence upon God and their obligation to their fellow men. Instead of regarding wealth as a talent to be employed for the glory of God and the uplifting of humanity, they look upon it as a means of serving themselves. Instead of developing in man the attributes of God, riches thus used are developing in him the attributes of Satan. The seed of the word is choked with thorns.

"And pleasures of this life." There is danger in amusement that is sought merely for self-gratification. All habits of indulgence that weaken the physical powers, that becloud the mind, or that benumb the spiritual perceptions, are "fleshly lusts, which war against the soul." 1 Peter 2:11.

"And the lusts of other things." These are not necessarily things sinful in themselves, but something that is made first instead of the kingdom of God. Whatever attracts the mind from God, whatever draws the affections away from Christ, is an enemy to the soul.

The Soil of Youthful Hearts

When the mind is youthful and vigorous and susceptible of rapid development, there is great temptation to be ambitious for self, to serve self. If worldly schemes are successful, there is an inclination to continue in a line that deadens conscience, and prevents a correct estimate as to what constitutes real excellence of character. When circumstances favor this development, growth will be seen in a direction prohibited by the word of God.

In this formative period of their children's life, the responsibility of parents is very great. It should be their study to surround the youth with

Whatever attracts the mind from God, whatever draws the affections away from Christ, is an enemy to the soul.

right influences, influences that will give them correct views of life and its true success. Instead of this, how many parents make it their first object to secure for their children worldly prosperity. All their associations are chosen with reference to this object. Many parents make their home in some large city, and introduce their children into fashionable society. They surround them with influences that encourage worldliness and pride. In this atmosphere the mind and soul are dwarfed. The high and noble aims of life are lost sight of. The privilege of being sons of God, heirs of eternity, is bartered for worldly gain.

Many parents seek to promote the happiness of their children by gratifying their love of amusement. They allow them to engage in sports and to attend parties of pleasure, and provide them with money to use freely in display and self-gratification. The more the desire for pleasure is indulged, the stronger it becomes. The interest of these youth is more and more absorbed in amusement, until they come to look upon it as the great object of life. They form habits of idleness and self-indulgence that make it almost impossible for them ever to become steadfast Christians.

The more the desire for pleasure is indulged, the stronger it becomes.

Even the church, which should be the pillar and ground of the truth, is found encouraging the selfish love of pleasure. When money is to be raised for religious purposes, to what means do many churches resort? To bazaars, suppers, fancy fairs, even to lotteries, and like devices. Often the place set apart for God's worship is desecrated by feasting and drinking, buying, selling, and merrymaking. Respect for the house of God and reverence for His worship are lessened in the minds of the youth. The barriers of self-restraint are weakened. Selfishness, appetite, the love of display, are appealed to, and they strengthen as they are indulged.

The pursuit of pleasure and amusement centers in the cities. Many parents who choose a city home for their children, thinking to give them greater advantages, meet with disappointment, and too late repent their terrible mistake. The cities of today are fast becoming like Sodom and Gomorrah. The many holidays encourage idleness. The exciting sports—theater-going, horse racing, gambling, liquor-drinking, and reveling—stimulate every passion to intense activity. The youth are swept away by the popular current. Those who learn to love amusement for its own sake open the door to a flood of temptations. They give themselves up to social gaiety and thoughtless mirth, and their intercourse with pleasure lovers has an intoxicating effect upon the mind. They are led on from one form of dissipation to another, until they lose both the desire and the capacity for a life of usefulness. Their religious aspirations are chilled; their spiritual life is darkened. All the nobler faculties of the soul, all that link man with the spiritual world, are debased.

It is true that some may see their folly and repent. God may pardon them. But they have wounded their own souls, and brought upon themselves a lifelong peril. The power of discernment, which ought ever to be kept keen and sensitive to distinguish between right and wrong, is in a great measure destroyed. They are not quick to recognize the guiding voice of the Holy Spirit, or to discern the devices of Satan. Too often in time of danger they fall under temptation, and are led away from God. The end of their pleasure-loving life is ruin for this world and for the world to come.

Cares, riches, pleasures—all are used by Satan in playing the game of life for the human soul. The warning is given, "Love not the world, neither the things that are in the world. If any man love the world, the love of the Father is not in him. For all that is in the world, the lust of the flesh, and the lust of the eyes, and the pride of life, is not of the Father, but is of the world." 1 John 2:15, 16. He who reads the hearts of men as an open book says, "Take heed to yourselves, lest at any time your hearts be overcharged with surfeiting, and drunkenness, and cares of this life." Luke 21:34. And the apostle Paul by the Holy Spirit writes, "They that will be rich fall into temptation and a snare, and into many foolish and hurtful lusts, which drown men in destruction and perdition. For the love of money is the root of all evil: which while some coveted after, they have erred from the faith, and pierced themselves through with many sorrows." 1 Timothy 6:9, 10.

Preparation of the Soil

Throughout the parable of the sower Christ represents the different results of the sowing as depending upon the soil. In every case the sower and the seed are the same. Thus He teaches that if the word of God fails of accomplishing its work in our hearts and lives, the reason is to be found in ourselves. But the result is not beyond our control. True, we cannot change ourselves; but the power of choice is ours, and it rests with us to determine what we will become. The wayside, the stony-ground, the thorny-ground hearers need not remain such. The Spirit of God is ever seeking to break the spell of infatuation that holds men absorbed in worldly things, and to awaken a desire for the imperishable treasure. It is by resisting the Spirit that men become inattentive to or neglectful of God's word. They are themselves responsible for the hardness of heart that prevents the good seed from taking root, and for the evil growths that check its development.

The garden of the heart must be cultivated. The soil must be broken up by deep repentance for sin. Poisonous, satanic plants must be uprooted. The soil once overgrown by thorns can be reclaimed only by diligent labor. So the evil tendencies of the natural heart can be overcome only by earnest effort in the name and strength of Jesus. The Lord bids us by His prophet, "Break up your fallow ground, and sow not among thorns." "Sow to yourselves in righteousness, reap in mercy." Jeremiah 4:3; Hosea 10:12. This work He desires to accomplish for us, and He asks us to cooperate with Him.

The sowers of the seed have a work to do in preparing hearts to receive the gospel. In the ministry of the word there is too much sermonizing and too little of real heart-to-heart work. There is need of personal labor for the souls of the lost. In Christlike sympathy we should come close to men individually, and seek to awaken their interest in the great things of eternal life. Their hearts may be as hard as the beaten highway, and apparently it may be a useless effort to present the Saviour to them; but while logic may fail to move, and argument be powerless to convince, the love of Christ, revealed in personal ministry, may soften the stony heart, so that the seed of truth can take root.

So the sowers have something to do that the seed may not be choked with thorns or perish because of shallowness of soil. At the very outset of the Christian life every believer should be taught its foundation principles. He should be taught that he is not merely to be saved by Christ's sacrifice, but that he is to make the life of Christ his life and the character of Christ his character. Let all be taught that they are to bear burdens and to deny natural inclination. Let them learn the blessedness of working for Christ, following Him in self-denial, and enduring hardness as good soldiers. Let them learn to trust His love and to cast on Him their cares. Let them taste the joy of winning souls for Him.

In their love and interest for the lost, they will lose sight of self. The pleasures of the world will lose their power to attract and its burdens to dishearten. The plowshare of truth will do its work. It will break up the fallow ground. It will not merely cut off the tops of the thorns, but will take them out by the roots.

In Good Ground

The sower is not always to meet with disappointment. Of the seed that fell into good ground the Saviour said, This "is he that heareth the word, and understandeth it; which also beareth fruit, and bringeth forth, some an hundredfold, some sixty, some thirty." "That on the good ground are they, which, in an honest and good heart, having heard the word, keep it, and bring forth fruit with patience."

God bids us fill the mind with great thoughts, pure thoughts.

The "honest and good heart" of which the parable speaks, is not a heart without sin; for the gospel is to be preached to the lost. Christ said, "I came not to call the righteous, but sinners to repentance." Mark 2:17. He has an honest heart who yields to the conviction of the Holy Spirit. He confesses his guilt, and feels his need of the mercy and love of God. He has a sincere desire to know the truth, that he may obey it. The good heart is a believing heart, one that has faith in the word of God. Without faith it is impossible to receive the word. "He that cometh to God must believe that He is, and that He is a rewarder of them that diligently seek Him." Hebrews 11:6.

This "is he that heareth the word, and understandeth it." The Pharisees of Christ's day closed their eyes lest they should see, and their ears lest they should hear; therefore the truth could not reach their hearts. They were to suffer retribution for their willful ignorance and self-imposed blindness. But Christ taught His disciples that they were to open their minds to instruction, and be ready to believe. He pronounced a blessing upon them because they saw and heard with eyes and ears that believed.

The good-ground hearer receives the word "not as the word of men, but as it is in truth, the word of God." 1 Thessalonians 2:13. Only he who receives the Scriptures as the voice of God speaking to himself is a true learner. He trembles at the word, for to him it is a living reality. He opens his understanding and his heart to receive it. Such hearers were Cornelius and his friends, who said to the apostle Peter, "Now therefore are we all here present before God, to hear all things that are commanded thee of God." Acts 10:33.

A knowledge of the truth depends not so much upon strength of intellect as upon pureness of purpose, the simplicity of an earnest, dependent faith. To those who in humility of heart seek for divine guidance, angels of God draw near. The Holy Spirit is given to open to them the rich treasures of the truth.

The good-ground hearers, having heard the word, keep it. Satan with all his agencies of evil is not able to catch it away.

Merely to hear or to read the word is not enough. He who desires to be profited by the Scriptures must meditate upon the truth that has been presented to him. By earnest attention and prayerful thought he must learn the meaning of the words of truth, and drink deep of the spirit of the holy oracles.

God bids us fill the mind with great thoughts, pure thoughts. He desires us to meditate upon His love and mercy, to study His wonderful work in the great plan of redemption. Then clearer and still clearer will be our perception of truth, higher, holier, our desire for purity of heart and clearness of thought. The soul dwelling in the pure atmosphere of holy thought will be transformed by communion with God through the study of the Scriptures.

"And bring forth fruit." Those who, having heard the word, keep it, will bring forth fruit in obedience. The word of God, received into the soul, will be manifest in good works. Its results will be seen in a Christlike character and life. Christ said of Himself, "I delight to do Thy will, O My God: yea, Thy law is within My heart." Psalm 40:8. "I seek not Mine own will, but the will of the Father which hath sent Me." John 5:30. And the Scripture says, "He that saith he abideth in Him ought himself also so to walk, even as He walked." 1 John 2:6.

The word of God often comes in collision with man's hereditary and cultivated traits of character and his habits of the good-ground hearer, in receiving the word, accepts all its conditions and requirements. His habits, customs, and practices are brought into submission to God's word. In his view the commands of finite, erring man sink into insignificance beside the word of the infinite God. With the whole heart, with undivided purpose, he is seeking the life eternal, and at the cost of loss, persecution, or death itself he will obey the truth.

And he brings forth fruit "with patience." None who receive God's word are exempt from difficulty and trial; but when affliction comes, the true Christian does not become restless, distrustful, or despondent. Though we cannot see the definite outcome of or discern the purpose of God's providences, we are not to cast away our confidence. Remembering the tender mercies of the Lord, we should cast our care upon Him, and with patience wait for His salvation.

Through conflict the spiritual life is strengthened. Trials well borne will develop steadfastness of character and precious spiritual graces. The perfect fruit of faith, meekness, and love often matures best amid storm clouds and darkness.

"The husbandman waiteth for the precious fruit of the earth, and hath long patience for it, until he receive the early and latter rain." James 5:7. So the Christian is to wait with patience for the fruition in his life of the word of God. Often when we pray for the graces of the Spirit, God works to answer our prayers by placing us in circumstances to develop these fruits; but we do not understand His purpose, and wonder and are dismayed. Yet none can develop these graces except through the process of growth and fruit bearing. Our part is to receive God's word and to hold it fast, yielding ourselves fully to its control, and its purpose in us will be accomplished.

"If a man love Me," Christ said, "he will keep My words: and My Father will love him, and we will come unto him, and make our abode with him." John 14:23. The spell of a stronger, a perfect mind will be over us; for we have a living connection with the source of all-enduring strength. In our divine life we shall be brought into captivity to Jesus Christ. We shall no longer live the common life of selfishness, but Christ will live in us. His character will be reproduced in our nature. Thus shall we bring forth the fruits of the Holy Spirit—"some thirty, and some sixty, and some an hundred."

"As the earth bringeth forth her bud, and as the garden causeth the things that are sown in it to spring forth; so the Lord God will cause righteousness and praise to spring forth" (Isa. 61:11).

Based on Mark 4:26-29

What Makes It Grow?

The parable of the sower excited much questioning. Some of the hearers gathered from it that Christ was not to establish an earthly kingdom, and many were curious and perplexed. Seeing their perplexity, Christ used other illustrations, still seeking to turn their thoughts from the hope of a worldly kingdom to the work of God's grace in the soul.

"And He said, So is the kingdom of God, as if a man should cast seed into the ground; and should sleep, and rise night and day, and the seed should spring and grow up, he knoweth not how. For the earth bringeth forth fruit of herself; first the blade, then the ear, after that the full corn in the ear. But when the fruit is brought forth, immediately he putteth in the sickle, because the harvest is come."

The husbandman who "putteth in the sickle, because the harvest is come," can be no other than Christ. It is He who at the last great day will reap the harvest of the earth. But the sower of the seed represents those who labor in Christ's stead. The seed is said to "spring and grow up, he knoweth not how," and this is not true of the Son of God. Christ does not sleep over His charge, but watches it day and night. He is not ignorant of how the seed grows.

The parable of the seed reveals that God is at work in nature. The seed has in itself a germinating principle, a principle that God Himself has implanted; yet if left to itself the seed would have no power to spring up. Man has his part to act in promoting the growth of the grain. He must prepare and enrich the soil and cast in the seed. He must till the fields. But there is a point beyond which he can accomplish nothing. No strength or wisdom of man can bring forth from the seed the living plant. Let man put forth his efforts to the utmost limit, he must still depend upon One who has connected the sowing and the reaping by wonderful links of His own omnipotent power.

There is life in the seed, there is power in the soil; but unless an infinite power is exercised day and night, the seed will yield no returns. The showers of rain must be sent to give moisture to the thirsty fields, the sun must impart heat, electricity must be conveyed to the buried seed. The life which the Creator has implanted, He alone can call forth. Every seed grows, every plant develops, by the power of God.

"As the earth bringeth forth her bud, and as the garden causeth the things that are sown in it to spring forth; so the Lord God will cause righteousness and praise to spring forth." Isaiah 61:11. As in the natural, so in the spiritual sowing; the teacher of truth must seek to prepare the soil of the heart; he must sow the seed; but the power that alone can produce life is from God. There is a point beyond which human effort is in vain. While we are to preach the word, we cannot impart the power that will quicken the soul, and cause righteousness and praise to spring forth. In the preaching of the word there must be the working of an agency beyond any human power. Only through the divine Spirit will the word be living and powerful to renew the soul unto eternal life. This is what Christ tried to impress upon His disciples. He taught that it was nothing they possessed in themselves which would give success to their labors, but that it is the miracle-working power of God which gives efficiency to His own word.

The work of the sower is a work of faith. The mystery of the germination and growth of the seed he cannot understand. But he has confidence in the agencies by which God causes vegetation to flourish. In casting his seed into the ground he is apparently throwing away the precious grain that might furnish bread for his family. But he is only giving up a present good for a larger return. He casts the seed away, expecting to gather it manyfold in an abundant harvest. So Christ's servants are to labor, expecting a harvest from the seed they sow.

The good seed may for a time lie unnoticed in a cold, selfish, worldly heart, giving no evidence that it has taken root; but afterward, as the Spirit of God breathes on the soul, the hidden seed springs up, and at last bears fruit to the glory of God. In our lifework we know not which shall prosper: this or that. This is not a question for us to settle. We are to do our work, and leave the results with God. "In the morning sow thy seed, and in the evening withhold not thine hand." Ecclesiastes 11:6. God's great covenant declares that "while the earth remaineth, seedtime and harvest . . . shall not cease." Genesis 8:22. In the confidence of this promise the husbandman tills and sows. Not less confidently are we in the spiritual sowing to labor, trusting His assurance, "So shall My word be that goeth forth out of My mouth: it shall not return unto Me void, but it shall accomplish that which I please, and it shall prosper in the thing whereto I sent it." Isaiah 55:11. "He that goeth forth and weepeth, bearing precious seed, shall doubtless come again with rejoicing, bringing his sheaves with him." Psalm 126:6.

The germination of the seed represents the beginning of spiritual life, and the development of the plant is a beautiful figure of Christian growth. As in nature, so in grace; there can be no life without growth. The plant must either grow or die. As its growth is silent and imperceptible, but continuous, so is the development of the Christian life. At every stage of development our life may be perfect; yet if God's purpose for us is fulfilled, there will be continual advancement. Sanctification is

It is the miracle-working power of God which gives efficiency to His own word.

the work of a lifetime. As our opportunities multiply, our experience will enlarge, and our knowledge increase. We shall become strong to bear responsibility, and our maturity will be in proportion to our privileges.

The plant grows by receiving that which God has provided to sustain its life. It sends down its roots into the earth. It drinks in the sunshine, the dew, and the rain. It receives the life-giving properties from the air. So the Christian is to grow by cooperating with the divine agencies. Feeling our helplessness, we are to improve all the opportunities granted us to gain a fuller experience. As the plant takes root in the soil, so we are to take deep root in Christ. As the plant receives the sunshine, the dew, and the rain, we are to open our hearts to the Holy Spirit. The work is to be done "not by might, nor by power, but by My spirit, saith the Lord of hosts." Zechariah 4:6. If we keep our minds stayed upon Christ, He will come unto us "as the rain, as the latter and former rain unto the earth." Hosea 6:3. As the Sun of Righteousness, He will arise upon us "with healing in His wings." Malachi 4:2. We shall "grow as the lily." We shall "revive as the corn, and grow as the vine." Hosea 14:5, 7. By constantly relying upon Christ as our personal Saviour, we shall grow up into Him in all things who is our head.

The wheat develops "first the blade, then the ear, after that the full corn in the ear." The object of the husbandman in the sowing of the seed and the culture of the growing plant is the production of grain. He desires bread for the hungry, and seed for future harvests. So the divine Husbandman looks for a harvest as the reward of His labor and sacrifice. Christ is seeking to reproduce Himself in the hearts of men; and He does this through those who believe in Him. The object of the Christian life is fruit bearing—the reproduction of Christ's character in the believer, that it may be reproduced in others.

The plant does not germinate, grow, or bring forth fruit for itself, but to "give seed to the sower, and bread to the eater." Isaiah 55:10. So no man is to live unto himself. The Christian is in the world as a representative of Christ, for the salvation of other souls.

There can be no growth or fruitfulness in the life that is centered in self. If you have accepted Christ as a personal Saviour, you are to forget yourself, and try to help others. Talk of the love of Christ, tell of His goodness. Do every duty that presents itself. Carry the burden of souls upon

As the plant receives the sunshine, the dew, and the rain, we are to open our hearts to the Holy Spirit.

your heart, and by every means in your power seek to save the lost. As you receive the Spirit of Christ—the Spirit of unselfish love and labor for others—you will grow and bring forth fruit. The graces of the Spirit will ripen in your character. Your faith will increase, your convictions deepen, your love be made perfect. More and more you will reflect the likeness of Christ in all that is pure, noble, and lovely.

"The fruit of the Spirit is love, joy, peace, longsuffering, gentleness, goodness, faith, meekness, temperance." Galatians 5:22, 23. This fruit can never perish, but will produce after its kind a harvest unto eternal life.

"When the fruit is brought forth, immediately

he putteth in the sickle, because the harvest is come." Christ is waiting with longing desire for the manifestation of Himself in His church. When the character of Christ shall be perfectly reproduced in His people, then He will come to claim them as His own.

It is the privilege of every Christian not only to look for but to hasten the coming of our Lord Jesus Christ. (2 Peter 3:12, margin.) Were all who profess His name bearing fruit to His glory, how quickly the whole world would be sown with the seed of the gospel. Quickly the last great harvest would be ripened, and Christ would come to gather the precious grain.

The plant grows by receiving that which God has provided to sustain its life. It sends down its roots into the earth. It drinks in the sunshine, the dew, and the rain. It receives the life-giving properties from the air. So the Christian is to grow by cooperating with the divine agencies. Feeling our helplessness, we are to improve all the opportunities granted us to gain a fuller experience. As the plant takes root in the soil, so we are to take deep root in Christ. As the plant receives the sunshine, the dew, and the rain, we are to open our hearts to the Holy Spirit. The work is to be done "not by might, nor by power, but by My spirit, saith the Lord of hosts." Zechariah 4:6. If we keep our minds stayed upon Christ, He will come unto us "as the rain, as the latter and former rain unto the earth." Hosea 6:3. As the Sun of Righteousness, He will arise upon us "with healing in His wings." Malachi 4:2. We shall "grow as the lily." We shall "revive as the corn, and grow as the vine." Hosea 14:5, 7. By constantly relying upon Christ as our personal Saviour, we shall grow up into Him in all things who is our head.

"The good seed are the children of the kingdom" (Matt. 13:38).

Based on Matthew 13:24-30, 37-43

WEEDS IN YOUR GARDEN

"Another parable put He forth unto them, saying, The kingdom of heaven is likened unto a man which sowed good seed in his field; but while men slept, his enemy came and sowed tares among the wheat, and went his way. But when the blade was sprung up, and brought forth fruit, then appeared the tares also."

"The field," Christ said, "is the world." But we must understand this as signifying the church of Christ in the world. The parable is a description of that which pertains to the kingdom of God, His work of salvation of men; and this work is accomplished through the church. True, the Holy Spirit has gone out into all the world; everywhere it is moving upon the hearts of men; but it is in the church that we are to grow and ripen for the garner of God.

"He that soweth the good seed is the Son of man; . . . the good seed are the children of the kingdom; but the tares are the children of the wicked one." The good seed represents those who are born of the word of God, the truth. The tares represent a class who are the fruit or embodiment of error, of false principles. "The enemy that sowed them is the devil." Neither God nor His angels ever sowed a seed that would produce a tare. The tares are always sown by Satan, the enemy of God and man.

In the East men sometimes took revenge upon an enemy by strewing his newly sown fields with the seeds of some noxious weed that, while growing, closely resembled wheat. Springing up with the wheat, it injured the crop and brought trouble and loss to the owner of the field. So it is from enmity to Christ that Satan scatters his evil seed among the good grain of the kingdom. The fruit of his sowing he attributes to the Son of God. By bringing into the church those who bear Christ's name while they deny His character, the wicked one causes that God shall be dishonored, the work of salvation misrepresented, and souls imperiled.

Christ's servants are grieved as they see true and false believers mingled in the church. They long to do something to cleanse the church. Like the servants of the householder, they are ready to uproot the tares. But Christ says to them, "Nay; lest while ye gather up the tares, ye root up also the wheat with them. Let both grow together until the harvest."

Christ has plainly taught that those who persist in open sin must be separated from the church, but He has not committed to us the work of judging character and motive. He knows our nature too well to entrust this work to us. Should we try to uproot from the church those whom we suppose to be spurious Christians, we should be sure to make mistakes. Often we regard as hopeless subjects the very ones whom

Often we regard as hopeless subjects the very ones whom Christ is drawing to Himself.

Christ is drawing to Himself. Were we to deal with these souls according to our imperfect judgment, it would perhaps extinguish their last hope. Many who think themselves Christians will at last be found wanting. Many will be in heaven who their neighbors supposed would never enter there. Man judges from appearance, but God judges the heart. The tares and the wheat are to grow together until the harvest, and the harvest is the end of probationary time.

There is in the Saviour's words another lesson, a lesson of wonderful forbearance and tender love. As the tares have their roots closely intertwined with those of the good grain, so false brethren in the church may be closely linked with true disciples. The real character of these pretended believers is not fully manifested. Were they to be separated from the church, others might be caused to stumble, who but for this would have remained steadfast.

The teaching of this parable is illustrated in God's own dealing with men and angels. Satan is a deceiver. When he sinned in heaven, even the loyal angels did not fully discern his character. This was why God did not at once destroy Satan. Had He done so, the holy angels would not have perceived the justice and love of God. A doubt of God's goodness would have been as evil seed that would yield the bitter fruit of sin and woe. Therefore the author of evil was spared, fully to develop his character. Through long ages God has borne the anguish of beholding the work of evil; He has given the infinite Gift of Calvary, rather than leave any to be deceived by the misrepresentations of the wicked one, for the tares could not be plucked up without danger of uprooting the precious grain. And shall we not be as forbearing toward our fellow men as the Lord of heaven and earth is toward Satan?

The world has no right to doubt the truth of Christianity because there are unworthy members in the church, nor should Christians become disheartened because of these false brethren. How was it with the early church? Ananias and Sapphira joined themselves to the disciples. Simon Magus was baptized. Demas, who forsook Paul, had been counted a believer. Judas Iscariot was numbered with the apostles. The Redeemer does not want to lose one soul; His experience with Judas is recorded to show His long patience with perverse human nature; and He bids us bear with it as He has borne. He has said that false brethren will be found in the church till the close of time.

Notwithstanding Christ's warning, men have sought to uproot the tares. To punish those who were supposed to be evildoers, the church has had recourse to the civil power. Those who differed from the established doctrines have been imprisoned, put to torture and to death, at the instigation of men who claimed to be acting under the sanction of Christ. But it is the spirit of Satan, not the Spirit of Christ, that inspires such acts. This is Satan's own method of bringing the world under his dominion. God has been misrepresented through the church by this way of dealing with those supposed to be heretics.

Not judgment and condemnation of others, but humility and distrust of self, is the teaching of Christ's parable. Not all that is sown in the field is good grain. The fact that men are in the church does not prove them Christians.

The tares closely resembled the wheat while the blades were green; but when the field was white for the harvest, the worthless weeds bore no likeness to the wheat that bowed under the weight of its full, ripe heads. Sinners who make a pretension of piety mingle for a time with the true followers of Christ, and the semblance of Christianity is calculated to deceive many; but in the harvest of the world there will be no likeness between good and evil. Then those who have joined the church, but who have not joined Christ, will be manifest.

The tares are permitted to grow among the wheat, to have all the advantage of sun and shower; but in the time of harvest ye shall "return, and discern between the righteous and the wicked, between him that serveth God and him that serveth Him not." Malachi 3:18. Christ Himself will decide who are worthy to dwell with the family of heaven. He will judge every man according to his words and his works. Profession is as nothing in the scale. It is character that decides destiny.

The Saviour does not point forward to a time when all the tares become wheat. The wheat and tares grow together until the harvest, the end of the world. Then the tares are bound in bundles to be burned, and the wheat is gathered into the garner of God. "Then shall the righteous shine forth as the sun in the kingdom of their Father." Then "the Son of man shall send forth His angels, and they shall gather out of His kingdom all things that offend, and them which do iniquity; and shall cast them into a furnace of fire: there shall be wailing and gnashing of teeth."

"Your faith should not stand in the wisdom of men,
but in the power of God" (I Cor. 2:5).

to trample down the growth springing from the same seed today? The old cry is repeated, "We *know* that God spake unto Moses: as for this fellow [Christ in the messenger He sends], we know not from whence he is." John 9:29. As in earlier ages, the special truths for this time are found, not with the ecclesiastical authorities, but with men and women who are not too learned or too wise to believe the word of God.

"For ye see your calling, brethren, how that not many wise men after the flesh, not many mighty, not many noble, are called: but God hath chosen the foolish things of the world to confound the wise; and God hath chosen the weak things of the world to confound the things which are mighty; and base things of the world, and things which are despised, hath God chosen, yea, and things which are not, to bring to nought things that are;" "that your faith should not stand in the wisdom of men, but in the power of God." 1 Corinthians 1:26-28; 2:5.

And in this last generation the parable of the mustard seed is to reach a signal and triumphant fulfillment. The little seed will become a tree. The last message of warning and mercy is to go to "every nation, and kindred, and tongue," "to take out of them a people for His name." Revelation 14:6-14; Acts 15:14. And the earth shall be lightened with His glory. (Revelation 18:1.)

"There is joy in the presence of the angels of God
over one sinner that repenteth"
(Luke 15:7).

PARTNERSHIP WITH POWER

From the work of seed sowing and the growth of the plant from the seed, precious lessons may be taught in the family and the school. Let the children and youth learn to recognize in natural things the working of divine agencies, and they will be enabled to grasp by faith unseen benefits. As they come to understand the wonderful work of God in supplying the wants of His great family, and how we are to cooperate with Him, they will have more faith in God, and will realize more of His power in their own daily life.

God created the seed, as He created the earth, by His word. By His word He gave it power to grow and multiply. He said, "Let the earth bring forth grass, the herb yielding seed, and the fruit tree yielding fruit after his kind, whose seed is in itself, upon the earth: and it was so. . . . And God saw that it was good." Genesis 1:11, 12. It is that word which still causes the seed to grow. Every seed that sends up its green blade to the sunlight declares the wonder-working power of that word uttered by Him who "spake, and it was," who "commanded, and it stood fast." Psalm 33:9.

Christ taught His disciples to pray, "Give us this day our daily bread." And pointing to the flowers He gave them the assurance, "If God so clothe the grass of the field, . . . shall He not much more clothe you?" Matthew 6:11, 30. Christ is constantly working to answer this prayer and to make good this assurance. There is an invisible power constantly at work as man's servant to feed and to clothe him. Many agencies our Lord employs to make the seed, apparently thrown away, a living plant. And He supplies in due proportion all that is required to perfect the harvest. In the beautiful words of the psalmist:

"Thou visitest the earth, and waterest it;
Thou greatly enrichest it;
The river of God is full of water:
Thou providest them corn, when Thou hast so prepared the earth.
Thou waterest her furrows abundantly;
Thou settlest the ridges thereof:
Thou makest it soft with showers;
Thou blessest the springing thereof.

Thou crownest the year with Thy
goodness;
And Thy paths drop fatness."
Psalm 65:9-11, R.V.

The material world is under God's control. The laws of nature are obeyed by nature. Everything speaks and acts the will of the Creator. Cloud and sunshine, dew and rain, wind and storm—all are under the supervision of God, and yield implicit obedience to His command. It is in obedience to the law of God that the spire of grain bursts through the ground, "first the blade, then the ear, after that the full corn in the ear." Mark 4:28.

Whenever man accomplishes anything, . . . he does it through cooperation with his Maker.

These the Lord develops in their proper season because they do not resist His working. And can it be that man made in the image of God, endowed with reason and speech, shall alone be unappreciative of His gifts and disobedient to His will? Shall rational beings alone cause confusion in our world?

In everything that tends to the sustenance of man is seen the concurrence of divine and human effort. There can be no reaping unless the human hand acts its part in the sowing of the seed. But without the agencies which God provides in giving sunshine and showers, dew and clouds, there would be no increase. Thus it is in every business pursuit, in every department of study and science. Thus it is in spiritual things, in the formation of the character, and in every line of Christian work. We have a part to act, but we must have the power of divinity to unite with us, or our efforts will be in vain.

Whenever man accomplishes anything, whether in spiritual or in temporal lines, he should bear in mind that he does it through cooperation with his Maker. There is great necessity for us to realize our dependence on God. Too much confidence is placed in man, too much reliance on human interventions. There is too little confidence in the power which God stands ready to give. "We are labourers together with God." 1 Corinthians 3:9. Immeasurably inferior is the part which the human agent sustains; but if he is linked with the divinity of Christ, he can do all things through the strength that Christ imparts.

The gradual development of the plant from the seed is an object lesson in child training. There is "first the blade, then the ear, after that the full corn in the ear." He who gave this parable created the tiny seed, gave it its vital properties, and ordained the laws that govern its growth. And the truths which the parable teaches were made a living reality in His own life. In both His physical and His spiritual nature He followed the divine order of growth illustrated by the plant, as He wishes all youth to do. Although He was the Majesty of heaven, the King of glory, He became a babe in Bethlehem, and for a time represented the helpless infant in its mother's care. In childhood He did the works of an obedient child. He spoke and acted with the wisdom of a child and not of a man, honoring His parents and carrying out their wishes in helpful ways, according to the ability of a child. But at each stage of His development He was perfect, with the simple natural grace of a sinless life. The sacred record says of His childhood, "The child grew, and waxed strong in spirit, filled with wisdom: and the grace of God was upon Him." And of His youth it is recorded, "Jesus increased in wisdom and stature, and in favour with God and man." Luke 2:40, 52.

The work of parents and teachers is here suggested. They should aim so to cultivate the tendencies of the youth that at each stage of their life they may represent the natural beauty appropriate to that period, unfolding naturally, as do the plants in the garden.

Those children are most attractive who are natural, unaffected. It is not wise to give them special notice and repeat their clever sayings before them. Vanity should not be encouraged by praising their looks, their words, or their actions. Nor should they be dressed in an expensive or showy manner. This encourages pride in them, and awakens envy in the hearts of their companions.

The little ones should be educated in childlike simplicity. They should be trained to be content with the small, helpful duties and the pleasures and experiences natural to their years. Childhood answers to the blade in the parable, and the blade has a beauty peculiarly its own. The children should not be forced into a precocious maturity but should retain as long as possible the freshness and grace of their early years.

The little children may be Christians, having an experience in accordance with their years. This is all that God expects of them. They need to be educated in spiritual things; and parents should give them every advantage that they may form characters after the similitude of the character of Christ.

In the laws of God in nature, effect follows cause with unerring certainty. The reaping will testify as to what the sowing has been. The slothful worker is condemned by his work. The harvest bears witness against him. So in spiritual things: the faithfulness of every worker is measured by the results of his work. The character of his work, whether diligent or slothful, is revealed by the harvest. It is thus that his destiny for eternity is decided.

Every seed sown produces a harvest of its kind. So it is in human life. We all need to sow the seeds of compassion, sympathy, and love; for we shall reap what we sow. Every characteristic of selfishness, self-love, self-esteem, every act of self-indulgence, will bring forth a like harvest. He who lives for self is sowing in the flesh, and of the flesh he will reap corruption.

Every seed sown produces a harvest of its kind. So it is in human life.

God destroys no man. Everyone who is destroyed will have destroyed himself. Everyone who stifles the admonitions of conscience is sowing the seeds of unbelief, and these will produce a sure harvest. By rejecting the first warning from God, Pharoah of old sowed the seeds of obstinacy, and he reaped obstinancy. God did not compel him to disbelieve. The seed of unbelief which he sowed produced a harvest of its kind. Thus his resistance continued, until he looked upon his devastated land, upon the cold, dead form of his first-born, and the first-born of all in his house and of all the families in his kingdom, until the waters of the sea closed over his horses and his chariots and his men of war. His history is a fearful illustration of the truth of the words that "whatsoever a man soweth, that shall he also reap." Galatians 6:7. Did men but realize this, they would be careful what seed they sow.

As the seed sown produces a harvest, and this in turn is sown, the harvest is multiplied. In our relation to others this law holds true. Every act, every word, is a seed that will bear fruit. Every deed of thoughtful kindness, of obedience, or of self-denial, will reproduce itself in others, and through them in still others. So every act of envy, malice, or dissension is a seed that will spring up in a "root of bitterness" (Hebrews 12:15), whereby many shall be defiled. And how much larger number will the "many" poison. Thus the sowing of good and evil goes on for time and eternity.

So in human life, to give is to live.

Liberality both in spiritual and in temporal things is taught in the lesson of seed sowing. The Lord says, "Blessed are ye that sow beside all waters." Isaiah 32:20. "This I say, He which soweth sparingly shall reap also sparingly; and he which soweth bountifully shall reap also bountifully." 2 Corinthians 9:6. To sow beside all waters means a continual imparting of God's gifts. It means giving wherever the cause of God or the needs of humanity demand our aid. This will not tend to poverty. "He which soweth bountifully shall reap also bountifully." The sower multiplies his seed by casting it away. So it is with those who are faithful in distributing God's gifts. By imparting they increase their blessings. God has promised them a sufficiency that they may continue to give. "Give, and it shall be given unto you; good measure, pressed down, and shaken together, and running over, shall men give into your bosom." Luke 6:38.

And more than this is wrapped up in the sowing and the reaping. As we distribute God's temporal blessings, the evidence of our love and sympathy awakens in the receiver gratitude and thanksgiving to God. The soil of the heart is prepared to receive the seeds of spiritual truth. And He who ministers seed to the sower will cause the seed to germinate and bear fruit unto eternal life.

By the casting of the grain into the soil Christ represents the sacrifice of Himself for our redemption. "Except a corn of wheat fall into the ground and die," He says, "it abideth alone: but if it die, it bringeth forth much fruit." John 12:24. So the death of Christ will result in fruit for the kingdom of God. In accordance with the law of the vegetable kingdom life will be the result of His death.

And all who would bring forth fruit as workers together with Christ must first fall into the ground and die. The life must be cast into the furrow of the world's need. Self-love, self-interest, must perish. But the law of self-sacrifice is the law of self-preservation. The seed buried in the ground produces fruit, and in turn this is planted. Thus the harvest is multiplied. The husbandman preserves his grain by casting it away. So in human life, to give is to live. The life that will be preserved is the life that is freely given in service to God and man. Those who for Christ's sake sacrifice their life in this world, will keep it unto life eternal.

The seed dies to spring forth into new life, and in this we are taught the lesson of the resurrection. All who love God will live again in the Eden above. Of the human body laid away to molder in the grave God has said, "It is sown in corruption; it is raised in incorruption: it is sown in dishonour;

it is raised in glory: it is sown in weakness; it is raised in power." 1 Corinthians 15:42, 43.

Such are a few of the many lessons taught by nature's living parable of the sower and the seed. As parents and teachers try to teach these lessons, the work should be made practical. Let the children themselves prepare the soil and sow the seed. As they work, the parent or teacher can explain the garden of the heart with the good or bad seed sown there, and that as the garden must be prepared for the natural seed, so the heart must be prepared for the seed of truth. As the seed is cast into the ground, they can teach the lesson of Christ's death; and as the blade springs up, they can teach the lesson of the truth of the resurrection. As the plants grow, the correspondence between the natural and the spiritual sowing may be continued.

The youth should be instructed in a similar way. They should be taught to till the soil. It would be well if there were, connected with every school, lands for cultivation. Such lands should be regarded as God's own schoolroom. The things of nature should be looked upon as a lesson book which His children are to study, and from which they may obtain knowledge as to the culture of the soul.

In tilling the soil, in disciplining and subduing the land, lessons may constantly be learned. No one would think of settling upon a raw piece of land, expecting it at once to yield a harvest. Earnestness, diligence, and persevering labor are to be put forth in treating the soil preparatory to sowing the seed. So it is in the spiritual work in the human heart. Those who would be benefited by the tilling of the soil must go forth with the word of God in their hearts. They will then find the fallow ground of the heart broken by the softening, subduing influence of the Holy Spirit. Unless hard work is bestowed on the soil, it will not yield a harvest. So with the soil of the heart: the Spirit of God must work upon it to refine and discipline it before it can bring forth fruit to the glory of God.

The soil will not produce its riches when worked by impulse. It needs thoughtful, daily attention. It must be plowed often and deep, with a view to keeping out the weeds that take nourishment from the good seed planted. Thus those who plow and sow prepare for the harvest. None need stand in the field amid the sad wreck of their hopes.

The blessing of the Lord will rest upon those who thus work the land, learning spiritual lessons from nature. In cultivating the soil the worker knows little what treasures will open up before him. While he is not to despise the instruction he may gather from minds that have had an experience, and from the information that intelligent men may impart, he should gather lessons for himself. This is a part of his training. The cultivation of the soil will prove an education to the soul.

Nature should be looked upon as a lesson book which His children are to study.

He who causes the seed to spring up, who tends it day and night, who gives it power to develop, is the Author of our being, the King of heaven, and He exercises still greater care and interest in behalf of His children. While the human sower is planting the seed to sustain our earthly life, the Divine Sower will plant in the soul the seed that will bring forth fruit unto life everlasting.

"He that spared not His own Son, but delivered Him up for us all, how shall He not with Him also freely give us all things?" (Rom. 8:32).

Based on Luke 18:1-8

GUARANTEED JUSTICE

Christ had been speaking of the period just before His second coming, and of the perils through which His followers must pass. With special reference to that time He related the parable "to this end, that men ought always to pray, and not to faint."

"There was in a city," He said, "a judge, which feared not God, neither regarded man: and there was a widow in that city; and she came unto him, saying, Avenge me of mine adversary. And he would not for a while: but afterward he said within himself, Though I fear not God, nor regard man; yet because this widow troubleth me, I will avenge her, lest by her continual coming she weary me. And the Lord said, Hear what the unjust judge saith. And shall not God avenge His own elect, which cry day and night unto Him, though He bear long with them? I tell you that He will avenge them speedily."

The judge who is here pictured had no regard for right, nor pity for suffering. The widow who pressed her case before him was persistently repulsed. Again and again she came to him, only to be treated with contempt, and to be driven from the judgment seat. The judge knew that her cause was righteous, and he could have relieved her at once, but he would not. He wanted to show his arbitrary power, and it gratified him to let her ask and plead and entreat in vain. But she would not fail nor become discouraged. Notwithstanding his indifference and hardheartedness, she pressed her petition until the judge consented to attend to her case. "Though I fear not God, nor regard man," he said, "yet because this widow troubleth me, I will avenge her, lest by her continual coming she weary me." To save his reputation, to avoid giving publicity to his partial, one-sided judgment, he avenged the persevering woman.

"And the Lord said, Hear what the unjust judge saith. And shall not God avenge His own elect, which cry day and night unto Him, though He bear long with them? I tell you that He will avenge them speedily." Christ here draws a sharp contrast between the unjust judge and God. The judge yielded to the widow's request merely through selfishness, that he might be relieved of her importunity. He felt for her no pity or compassion; her misery was nothing to him. How different is the attitude of God toward those who seek Him. The appeals of the needy and distressed are considered by Him with infinite compassion.

The woman who entreated the judge for justice had lost her husband by death. Poor and friendless, she had no means of retrieving her ruined fortunes. So by sin, man lost his connection with God. Of himself he has no means of salvation. But in Christ we are brought nigh unto the Father. The elect of God are dear to His heart. They are those whom He has called out of darkness into His marvelous light, to show forth His praise, to shine as lights amid the darkness of the world. The unjust judge had no special interest in the widow who importuned him for deliverance; yet in order to rid himself of her pitiful appeals, he heard her plea, and delivered her from her adversary. But God loves His children with infinite love. To Him the dearest object on earth is His church.

The work of Satan as an accuser began in heaven. This has been his work on earth ever since man's fall.

"For the Lord's portion is His people; Jacob is the lot of His inheritance. He found him in a desert land, and in the waste howling wilderness; He led him about, He instructed him, He kept him as the apple of His eye." Deuteronomy 32:9, 10. "For thus saith the Lord of hosts; After the glory hath He sent Me unto the nations which spoiled you: for he that toucheth you toucheth the apple of His eye." Zechariah 2:8.

The widow's prayer, "Avenge me"—"do me justice" (R.V.)—"of mine adversary," represents the prayer of God's children. Satan is their great adversary. He is the "accuser of our brethren," who accuses them before God day and night. (Revelation 12:10.) He is continually working to misrepresent and accuse, to deceive and destroy the people of God. And it is for deliverance from the power of Satan and his agents that in this parable Christ teaches His disciples to pray.

In the prophecy of Zechariah is brought to view Satan's accusing work, and the work of Christ in resisting the adversary of His people. The prophet says, "He shewed me Joshua the high priest standing before the angel of the Lord, and Satan standing at his right hand to resist him. And the Lord said unto Satan, The Lord rebuke thee, O Satan; even the Lord that hath chosen Jerusalem rebuke thee: is not this a brand plucked out of the fire? Now Joshua was clothed with filthy garments, and stood before the angel." Zechariah 3:1-3.

The people of God are here represented as a criminal on trial. Joshua, as high priest, is seeking for a blessing for his people, who are in great affliction. While he is pleading before God, Satan is standing at his right hand as his adversary. He is accusing the children of God, and making their case appear as desperate as possible. He presents before the Lord their evil doings and their defects. He shows their faults and failures, hoping they will appear of such a character in the eyes of Christ that He will render them no help in their great need. Joshua, as the representative of God's people, stands under condemnation, clothed with filthy garments. Aware of the sins of his people, he is weighed down with discouragement. Satan is pressing upon his soul a sense of guiltiness that makes him feel almost hopeless. Yet there he stands as a suppliant, with Satan arrayed against him.

The work of Satan as an accuser began in heaven. This has been his work on earth ever since man's fall, and it will be his work in a special sense as we approach nearer to the close of this world's history. As he sees that his time is short, he will work with greater earnestness to deceive and destroy. He is angry when he sees a people on the earth who, even in their weakness and sinfulness, have respect to the law of Jehovah. He is determined that they shall not obey God. He delights in their unworthiness, and has devices prepared for every soul, that all may be ensnared and separated from God. He seeks to accuse and condemn God and all who strive to carry out His purposes in this world in mercy and love, in compassion and forgiveness.

Every manifestation of God's power for His people arouses the enmity of Satan. Every time God works in their behalf, Satan with his angels works with renewed vigor to compass their ruin. He is jealous of all who make Christ their strength. His object is to instigate evil, and when he has succeeded, throw all the blame upon the tempted ones. He points to their filthy garments, their defective characters. He presents their weakness and folly, their sins of ingratitude, their unlikeness to Christ, which have dishonored their Redeemer. All this he urges as an argument proving his right to work his will in their destruction. He endeavors to affright their souls with the thought that their case is hopeless, that the stain of their defilement can never be washed away. He hopes so to destroy their faith that they will yield fully to his temptations and turn from their allegiance to God.

The Lord's people cannot of themselves answer the charges of Satan. As they look to themselves they are ready to despair. But they appeal to the divine Advocate. They plead the merits of the Redeemer. God can be "just, and the justifier of him which believeth in Jesus." Romans 3:26. With confidence the Lord's children cry unto Him to silence the accusations of Satan, and bring to nought his devices. "Do me justice of mine adversary," they pray; and with the mighty argument of the cross Christ silences the bold accuser.

"The Lord said unto Satan, The Lord rebuke thee, O Satan; even the Lord that hath chosen

Every manifestation of God's power for His people arouses the enmity of Satan.

Jerusalem rebuke thee: is not this a brand plucked out of the fire?" When Satan seeks to cover the people of God with blackness, and ruin them, Christ interposes. Although they have sinned Christ has taken the guilt of their sins upon His own soul. He has snatched the race as a brand from the fire. By His human nature He is linked with man, while through His divine nature He is one with the infinite God. Help is brought within the reach of perishing souls. The adversary is rebuked.

"Now Joshua was clothed with filthy garments, and stood before the angel. And he answered and spake unto those that stood before him, saying, Take away the filthy garments from him. And unto him he said, Behold, I have caused thine iniquity to pass from thee, and I will clothe thee with change of raiment. And I said, Let them set a fair mitre upon his head. So they set a fair mitre upon his head, and clothed him with garments." Then with the authority of the Lord of hosts the angel made a solemn pledge to Joshua, the representative of God's people: "If thou wilt walk in My ways, and if thou wilt keep My charge, then thou shalt also judge My house, and shalt also keep My courts, and I will give thee places to walk among these that stand by"—even among the angels that surround the throne of God. (Zechariah 3:3-7.)

Satan . . . is shown to be an accuser and deceiver. God will do justice for His own elect.

Notwithstanding the defects of the people of God, Christ does not turn away from the objects of His care. He has the power to change their raiment. He removes the filthy garments; He places upon the repenting, believing ones His own robe of righteousness, and writes pardon against their names on the records of heaven. He confesses them as His before the heavenly universe. Satan, their adversary, is shown to be an accuser and deceiver. God will do justice for His own elect.

The prayer, "Do me justice of mine adversary," applies not only to Satan but to the agencies whom he instigates to misrepresent, to tempt, and to destroy the people of God. Those who have decided to obey the commandments of God will understand by experience that they have adversaries who are controlled by a power from beneath. Such adversaries beset Christ at every step, how constantly and determinedly no human being can ever know. Christ's disciples, like their Master, are followed by continual temptation.

The Scriptures describe the condition of the world just before Christ's second coming. James the apostle pictures the greed and oppression that will prevail. He says, "Go to now, ye rich men. . . . Ye have heaped treasure together for the last days. Behold, the hire of the labourers who have reaped down your fields, which is of you kept back by fraud, crieth: and the cries of them which have reaped are entered into the ears of the Lord of sabaoth. Ye have lived in pleasure on the earth, and been wanton; ye have nourished your hearts, as in a day of slaughter. Ye have condemned and killed the just; and he doth not resist you." James 5:1-6. This is a picture of what exists today. By every species of oppression and extortion, men are piling up colossal fortunes, while the cries of starving humanity are coming up before God.

"Judgment is turned away backward, and justice standeth afar off: for truth is fallen in the street, and equity cannot enter. Yea, truth faileth; and he that departeth from evil maketh himself a prey." Isaiah 59:14, 15. This was fulfilled in the life of Christ on earth. He was loyal to God's commandments, setting aside the human traditions and requirements which had been exalted in their place. Because of this He was hated and persecuted. This history is repeated. The laws and traditions of men are exalted above the law of God, and those who are true to God's commandments suffer reproach and persecution. Christ, because of His faithfulness to God, was accused as a Sabbathbreaker and blasphemer. He was declared to be possessed of a devil, and was denounced as Beelzebub. In like manner His followers are accused and misrepresented. Thus Satan hopes to lead them to sin, and cast dishonor upon God.

The character of the judge in the parable, who feared not God nor regarded man, was presented by Christ to show the kind of judgment that was then being executed, and that would soon be witnessed at His trial. He desires His people in all time to realize how little dependence can be placed on earthly rulers or judges in the day of adversity. Often the elect people of God have to stand before men in official positions who do not make the word of God their guide and counselor, but who follow their own unconsecrated, undisciplined impulses.

In the parable of the unjust judge Christ has shown what we should do. "Shall not God avenge His own elect, which cry day and night unto Him?" Christ, our example, did nothing to vindicate or deliver Himself. He committed His case to God. So His followers are not to accuse or condemn, or to resort to force in order to deliver themselves.

When trials arise that seem unexplainable, we should not allow our peace to be spoiled. However unjustly we may be treated, let not passion arise. By indulging a spirit of retaliation we injure ourselves. We destroy our own confidence in God, and grieve the Holy Spirit. There is by our side a witness, a heavenly messenger, who will lift up for us a standard against the enemy. He will shut us in with the bright beams of the Sun of Righteousness. Beyond this, Satan cannot penetrate. He cannot pass this shield of holy light.

While the world is progressing in wickedness, none of us need flatter ourselves that we shall have no difficulties. But it is these very difficulties that bring us into the audience chamber of the Most High. We may seek counsel of One who is infinite in wisdom.

The Lord says, "Call upon Me in the day of trouble." Psalm 50:15. He invites us to present to Him our perplexities and necessities, and our need of divine help. He bids us be instant in prayer. As soon as difficulties arise, we are to offer to Him our sincere, earnest petitions. By our importunate prayers we give evidence of our strong confidence in God. The sense of our need leads us to pray earnestly, and our heavenly Father is moved by our supplications.

Often those who suffer reproach or persecution for their faith are tempted to think themselves forsaken by God. In the eyes of men they are in the minority. To all appearance their enemies triumph over them. But let them not violate their conscience. He who has suffered in their behalf, and has borne their sorrows and afflictions, has not forsaken them.

As soon as difficulties arise, we are to offer to Him our sincere, earnest petitions.

The children of God are not left alone and defenseless. Prayer moves the arm of Omnipotence. Prayer has "subdued kingdoms, wrought righteousness, obtained promises, stopped the mouths of lions, quenched the violence of fire"—we shall know what it means when we hear the reports of the martyrs who died for their faith—"turned to flight the armies of the aliens." Hebrews 11:33, 34.

If we surrender our lives to His service, we can never be placed in a position for which God has not made provision. Whatever may be our situation, we have a Guide to direct our way; whatever our perplexities, we have a sure Counselor; whatever our sorrow, bereavement, or loneliness, we have a sympathizing Friend. If in our ignorance we make missteps, Christ does not leave us. His voice, clear and distinct, is heard saying, "I am the way, the truth, and the life." John 14:6. "He shall deliver the needy when he crieth; the poor also, and him that hath no helper." Psalm. 72:12.

Not one sincere prayer is lost. Amid the anthems of the celestial choir God hears the cries of the weakest human being.

The Lord declares that He will be honored by those who draw nigh to Him, who faithfully do His service. "Thou wilt keep him in perfect peace, whose mind is stayed on Thee: because he trusteth in Thee." Isaiah 26:3. The arm of Omnipotence is outstretched to lead us onward and still onward. Go forward, the Lord says; I will send you help. It is for My name's glory that you ask, and you shall receive. I will be honored before those who are watching for your failure. They shall see My word triumph gloriously. "All things, whatsoever ye shall ask in prayer, believing, ye shall receive." Matthew 21:22.

Let all who are afflicted or unjustly used, cry to God. Turn away from those whose hearts are as steel, and make your requests known to your Maker. Never is one repulsed who comes to Him with a contrite heart. Not one sincere prayer is lost. Amid the anthems of the celestial choir God hears the cries of the weakest human being. We pour out our heart's desire in our closets, we breathe a prayer as we walk by the way, and our words reach the throne of the Monarch of the universe. They may be inaudible to any human ear, but they cannot die away into silence, nor can they be lost through the activities of business that are going on. Nothing can drown the soul's desire. It rises above the din of the street, above the confusion of the multitude, to the heavenly courts. It is God to whom we are speaking, and our prayer is heard.

You who feel the most unworthy, fear not to commit your case to God. When He gave Himself in Christ for the sin of the world, He undertook the case of every soul. "He that spared not His own Son, but delivered Him up for us all, how shall He not with Him also freely give us all things?" Romans 8:32. Will He not fulfill the gracious word given for our encouragement and strength?

Christ desires nothing so much as to redeem His heritage from the dominion of Satan. But before we are delivered from Satan's power without, we must be delivered from his power within. The Lord permits trials in order that we may be cleansed from earthliness, from selfishness, from harsh, unchristlike traits of character. He suffers the deep waters of affliction to go over our souls in order that we may know Him and Jesus Christ whom He has sent, in order that we may have deep heart longings to be cleansed from defilement, and may come forth from the trial purer, holier, happier. Often we enter the furnace of trial with our souls dark-

know that the last great crisis is at hand. When the defiance of God's law is almost universal, when His people are oppressed and afflicted by their fellow men, the Lord will interpose.

The time is near when He will say, "Come, My people, enter thou into thy chambers, and shut thy doors about thee: hide thyself as it were for a little moment, until the indignation be overpast. For, behold, the Lord cometh out of His place to punish the inhabitants of the earth for their iniquity: the earth also shall disclose her blood, and shall no more cover her slain." Isaiah 26:20, 21. Men who claim to be Christians may now defraud and oppress the poor; they may rob the widow and fatherless; they may indulge their satanic hatred because they cannot control the consciences of God's people; but for all this God will bring them into judgment. They "shall have judgment without mercy" that have "shewed no mercy." James 2:13. Not long hence they will stand before the Judge of all the earth, to render an account for the pain they have caused to the bodies and souls of His heritage. They may now indulge in false accusations, they may deride those whom God has appointed to do His work, they may consign His believing ones to prison, to the chain gang, to banishment, to death; but for every pang of anguish, every tear shed, they must answer. God will reward them double for their sins. Concerning Babylon, the symbol of the apostate church, He says to His ministers of judgment, "Her sins have reached unto heaven, and God hath remembered her iniquities. Reward her even as she rewarded you, and double unto her double according to her works: in the cup which she hath filled fill to her double." Revelation 18:5, 6.

From India, from Africa, from China, from the islands of the sea, from the downtrodden millions of so-called Christian lands, the cry of human woe is ascending to God. That cry will not long be unanswered. God will cleanse the earth from its moral corruption, not by a sea of water as in Noah's day, but by a sea of fire that cannot be quenched by any human devising.

"There shall be a time of trouble, such as never was since there was a nation even to that same time: and at that time Thy people shall be delivered, every one that shall be found written in the book." Daniel 12:1.

From garrets, from hovels, from dungeons, from scaffolds, from mountains and deserts, from the caves of the earth and the caverns of the sea, Christ will gather His children to Himself. On earth they have been destitute, afflicted, and tormented. Millions have gone down to the grave loaded with infamy because they refused to yield to the deceptive claims of Satan. By human tribunals the children of God have been adjudged the vilest criminals. But the day is near when "God is judge Himself." Psalm 50:6. Then the decisions of earth shall be reversed. "The rebuke of His people shall He take away." Isaiah 25:8. White robes will be given to every one of them. (Revelation 6:11.) And "they shall call them, The holy people, The redeemed of the Lord." Isaiah 62:12.

Whatever crosses they have been called to bear, whatever losses they have sustained, whatever persecution they have suffered, even to the loss of their temporal life, the children of God are amply recompensed. "They shall see His face; and His name shall be in their foreheads." Revelation 22:4.

"I have gone astray like a lost sheep; seek Thy servant" (Ps. 119:176).

Based on Luke 15:1-10

THE LITTLE LOST LAMB

As the "publicans and sinners" gathered about Christ, the rabbis expressed their displeasure. "This man receiveth sinners," they said, "and eateth with them."

By this accusation they insinuated that Christ liked to associate with the sinful and vile, and was insensible to their wickedness. The rabbis had been disappointed in Jesus. Why was it that one who claimed so lofty a character did not mingle with them and follow their methods of teaching? Why did He go about so unpretendingly, working among all classes? If He were a true prophet, they said, He would harmonize with them, and would treat the publicans and sinners with the indifference they deserved. It angered these guardians of society that He with whom they were continually in controversy, yet whose purity of life awed and condemned them, should meet, in such apparent sympathy, with social outcasts. They did not approve of His methods. They regarded themselves as educated, refined, and pre-eminently religious; but Christ's example laid bare their selfishness.

It angered them also that those who showed only contempt for the rabbis and who were never seen in the synagogues should flock about Jesus and listen with rapt attention to His words. The scribes and Pharisees felt only condemnation in that pure presence; how was it, then, that publicans and sinners were drawn to Jesus?

They knew not that the explanation lay in the very words they had uttered as a scornful charge, "This man receiveth sinners." The souls who came to Jesus felt in His presence that even for them there was escape from the pit of sin. The Pharisees had only scorn and condemnation for them; but Christ greeted them as children of God, estranged indeed from the Father's house, but not forgotten by the Father's heart. And their very misery and sin made them only the more the objects of His compassion. The farther they had wandered from Him, the more earnest the longing and the greater the sacrifice for their rescue.

All this the teachers of Israel might have learned from the sacred scrolls of which it was their pride to be the keepers and expounders.

Had not David written—David, who had fallen into deadly sin—"I have gone astray like a lost sheep; seek Thy servant"? Psalm 119:176. Had not Micah revealed God's love to the sinner, saying, "Who is a God like unto Thee, that pardoneth iniquity, and passeth by the transgression of the remnant of His heritage? He retaineth not His anger for ever, because He delighteth in mercy"? Micah 7:18.

The Lost Sheep

Christ did not at this time remind His hearers of the words of Scripture. He appealed to the witness of their own experience. The widespreading tablelands on the east of Jordan afforded abundant pasturage for flocks, and through the gorges and over the wooded hills had wandered many a lost sheep, to be searched for and brought back by the shepherd's care. In the company about Jesus there were shepherds, and also men who had money invested in flocks and herds, and all could appreciate His illustration: "What man of *you*, having an hundred sheep, if he lose one of them, doth not leave the ninety and nine in the wilderness, and go after that which is lost, until he find it?"

So if there had been but one lost soul, Christ would have died for that one.

These souls whom you despise, said Jesus, are the property of God. By creation and by redemption they are His, and they are of value in His sight. As the shepherd loves his sheep, and cannot rest if even one be missing, so, in an infinitely higher degree, does God love every outcast soul. Men may deny the claim of His love, they may wander from Him, they may choose another master; yet they are God's, and He longs to recover His own. He says, "As a shepherd seeketh out his flock in the day that he is among his sheep that are scattered; so will I seek out My sheep, and will deliver them out of all places where they have been scattered in the cloudy and dark day." Ezekiel 34:12.

In the parable the shepherd goes out to search for one sheep—the very least that can be numbered. So if there had been but one lost soul, Christ would have died for that one.

The sheep that has strayed from the fold is the most helpless of all creatures. It must be sought for by the shepherd, for it cannot find its way back. So with the soul that has wandered away from God; he is as helpless as the lost sheep, and unless divine love had come to his rescue he could never find his way to God.

The shepherd who discovers that one of his sheep is missing does not look carelessly upon the flock that is safely housed, and say, "I have ninety and nine, and it will cost me too much trouble to go in search of the straying one. Let him come back, and I will open the door of the sheepfold, and let him in." No; no sooner does the sheep go astray than the shepherd is filled with grief and anxiety. He counts and recounts the flock. When he is sure that one sheep is lost, he slumbers not. He leaves the ninety and nine within the fold, and goes in search of the straying sheep. The darker and more tempestuous the night and the more perilous the way, the greater is the shepherd's anxiety and the more earnest his search. He makes every effort to find that one lost sheep.

With what relief he hears in the distance its

first faint cry. Following the sound, he climbs the steepest heights; he goes to the very edge of the precipice, at the risk of his own life. Thus he searches, while the cry, growing fainter, tells him that his sheep is ready to die. At last his effort is rewarded; the lost is found. Then he does not scold it because it has caused him so much trouble. He does not drive it with a whip. He does not even try to lead it home. In his joy he takes the trembling creature upon his shoulders; if it is bruised and wounded, he gathers it in his arms, pressing it close to his bosom, that the warmth of his own heart may give it life. With gratitude that his search has not been in vain, he bears it back to the fold.

Thank God, He has presented to our imagination no picture of a sorrowful shepherd returning without the sheep. The parable does not speak of failure but of success and joy in the recovery. Here is the divine guarantee that not even one of the straying sheep of God's fold is overlooked, not one is left unsuccored. Every one that will submit to be ransomed, Christ will rescue from the pit of corruption and from the briers of sin.

Desponding soul, take courage, even though you have done wickedly. Do not think that *perhaps* God will pardon your transgressions and permit you to come into His presence. God has made the first advance. While you were in rebellion against Him, He went forth to seek you. With the tender heart of the shepherd He left the ninety and nine, and went out into the wilderness to find that which was lost. The soul, bruised and wounded and ready to perish, He encircles in His arms of love and joyfully bears it to the fold of safety.

It was taught by the Jews that before God's love is extended to the sinner, he must first repent. In their view repentance is a work by which men earn the favor of Heaven. And it was this thought that led the Pharisees to exclaim in astonishment and anger, "This man receiveth sinners." According to their ideas He should permit none to approach Him but those who had repented. But in the parable of the lost sheep Christ teaches that salvation does not come through our seeking after God but through God's seeking after us. "There is none that understandeth, there is none that seeketh after God. They are all gone out of the way." Romans 3:11, 12. We do not repent in order that God may love us, but He reveals to us His love in order that we may repent.

God has made the first advance. While you were in rebellion against Him, He went forth to seek you.

When the straying sheep is at last brought home, the shepherd's gratitude finds expression in melodious songs of rejoicing. He calls upon his friends and neighbors, saying unto them, "Rejoice with me; for I have found my sheep which was lost." So when a wanderer is found by the great Shepherd of the sheep, heaven and earth unite in thanksgiving and rejoicing.

"Joy shall be in heaven over one sinner that repenteth, more than over ninety and nine just persons, which need no repentance." You Pharisees, said Christ, regard yourselves as the favorites of heaven. You think yourselves secure in your own righteousness. Know, then, that if you need no repentance, My mission is not to you. These poor souls who feel their poverty and sinfulness are the very ones whom I have come to rescue. Angels of heaven are interested in these lost ones whom you despise. You complain and sneer when one of these souls joins himself to Me; but know that angels rejoice, and the song of triumph rings through the courts above.

The rabbis had a saying that there is rejoicing in heaven when one who has sinned against God is destroyed; but Jesus taught that to God the work of destruction is a strange work. That in which all heaven delights is the restoration of God's own image in the souls whom He has made.

In every assembly for worship, there are souls longing for rest and peace.

When one who has wandered far in sin seeks to return to God, he will encounter criticism and distrust. There are those who will doubt whether his repentance is genuine, or will whisper, "He has no stability; I do not believe that he will hold out." These persons are doing not the work of God but the work of Satan, who is the accuser of the brethren. Through their criticisms the wicked one hopes to discourage that soul, and to drive him still farther from God. Let the repenting sinner contemplate the rejoicing in heaven over the return of the one that was lost. Let him rest in the love of God and in no case be disheartened by the scorn and suspicion of the Pharisees.

The rabbis understood Christ's parable as applying to the publicans and sinners; but it has also a wider meaning. By the lost sheep Christ represents not only the individual sinner but the one world that has apostatized and has been ruined by sin. This world is but an atom in the vast dominions over which God presides, yet this little fallen world—the one lost sheep—is more precious in His sight than are the ninety and nine that went not astray from the fold. Christ, the loved Commander in the heavenly courts, stooped from His high estate, laid aside the glory that He had with the Father, in order to save the one lost world. For this He left the sinless worlds on high, the ninety and nine that loved Him, and came to this earth, to be "wounded for our transgressions" and "bruised for our iniquities." Isaiah 53:5. God gave Himself in His Son that He might have the joy of receiving back the sheep that was lost.

"Behold, what manner of love the Father hath bestowed upon us, that we should be called the sons of God." 1 John 3:1. And Christ says, "As Thou hast sent Me into the world, even so have I also sent them into the world" (John 17:18)—to "fill up that which is behind of the afflictions of Christ . . . for His body's sake, which is the church." Colossians 1:24. Every soul whom Christ has rescued is called to work in His name for the saving of the lost. This work had been neglected in Israel. Is it not neglected today by those who profess to be Christ's followers?

How many of the wandering ones have you, reader, sought for and brought back to the fold? When you turn from those who seem unpromising and unattractive, do you realize that you are neglecting the souls for whom Christ is seeking?

At the very time when you turn from them, they may be in the greatest need of your compassion. In every assembly for worship, there are souls longing for rest and peace. They may appear to be living careless lives, but they are not insensible to the influence of the Holy Spirit. Many among them might be won for Christ.

If the lost sheep is not brought back to the fold, it wanders until it perishes. And many souls go down to ruin for want of a hand stretched out to save. These erring ones may appear hard and reckless; but if they had received the same advantages that others have had, they might have revealed far more nobility of soul, and greater talent for usefulness. Angels pity these wandering ones. Angels weep, while human eyes are dry and hearts are closed to pity.

O the lack of deep, soul-touching sympathy for the tempted and the erring! O for more of Christ's spirit, and for less, far less, of self!

The Pharisees understood Christ's parable as a rebuke to them. Instead of accepting their criticism of His work, He had reproved their neglect of the publicans and sinners. He had not done this openly, lest it should close their hearts against Him; but His illustration set before them the very work which God required of them, and which they had failed to do. Had they been true shepherds, these leaders in Israel would have done the work of a shepherd. They would have manifested the mercy and love of Christ, and would have united with Him in His mission. Their refusal to do this had proved their claims of piety to be false. Now many rejected Christ's reproof; yet to some His words brought conviction. Upon these, after Christ's ascension to heaven, the Holy Spirit came, and they united with His disciples in the very work outlined in the parable of the lost sheep.

The Lost Piece of Silver

After giving the parable of the lost sheep Christ spoke another, saying "What woman having ten pieces of silver, if she lose one piece, doth not light a candle, and sweep the house, and seek diligently till she find it?"

In the East the houses of the poor usually consisted of but one room, often windowless and dark. The room was rarely swept, and a piece of money falling on the floor would be speedily covered by the dust and rubbish. In order that it might be found, even in the daytime, a candle must be lighted, and the house must be swept diligently.

The wife's marriage portion usually consisted of pieces of money, which she carefully preserved as her most cherished possession, to be transmitted to her own daughters. The loss of one of these pieces would be regarded as a serious calamity, and its recovery would cause great rejoicing, in which the neighboring women would readily share.

The lost coin represents those who are lost in . . . sins, but . . . have no sense of their condition.

"When she hath found it," Christ said, "she calleth her friends and her neighbors together, saying, Rejoice with me; for I have found the piece which I had lost. Likewise, I say unto you, there is joy in the presence of the angels of God over one sinner that repenteth."

This parable, like the preceding, sets forth the loss of something which with proper search may be recovered, and that with great joy. But the two parables represent different classes. The lost sheep knows that it is lost. It has left the shepherd and the flock, and it cannot recover itself. It represents those who realize that they are separated from God and who are in a cloud of perplexity, in humiliation, and sorely tempted. The lost coin represents those who are lost in trespasses and sins, but who have no sense of their condition. They are estranged from God, but they know it not. Their souls are in peril, but they are unconscious and unconcerned. In this parable Christ teaches that even those who are indifferent to the claims of God are the objects of His pitying love. They are to be sought for that they may be brought back to God.

So every soul, however degraded by sin, is in God's sight accounted precious.

The sheep wandered away from the fold; it was lost in the wilderness or upon the mountains. The piece of silver was lost in the house. It was close at hand, yet it could be recovered only by diligent search.

This parable has a lesson to families. In the household there is often great carelessness concerning the souls of its members. Among their number may be one who is estranged from God; but how little anxiety is felt lest in the family relationship there be lost one of God's entrusted gifts.

The coin, though lying among dust and rubbish, is a piece of silver still. Its owner seeks it because it is of value. So every soul, however degraded by sin, is in God's sight accounted precious. As the coin bears the image and superscription of the reigning power, so man at his creation bore the image and superscription of God; and though now marred and dim through the influence of sin, the traces of this inscription remain upon every soul. God desires to recover that soul and to retrace upon it His own image in righteousness and holiness.

The woman in the parable searches diligently for her lost coin. She lights the candle and sweeps the house. She removes everything that might obstruct her search. Though only one piece is lost, she will not cease her efforts until that piece is found. So in the family, if one member is lost to God, every means should be used for his recovery. On the part of all the others let there be diligent, careful self-examination. Let the life-practice be investigated. See if there is not some mistake, some error in management, by which that soul is confirmed in impenitence.

If there is in the family one child who is unconscious of his sinful state, parents should not rest. Let the candle be lighted. Search the word of God, and by its light let everything in the home be diligently examined, to see why this child is lost. Let parents search their own hearts, examine their habits and practices. Children are the heritage of the Lord, and we are answerable to Him for our management of His property.

There are fathers and mothers who long to labor in some foreign mission field; there are many who are active in Christian work outside the home, while their own children are strangers to the Saviour and His love. The work of winning their children for Christ many parents trust to the minister or the Sabbath school teacher, but in doing this they are neglecting their own God-given responsibility. The education and training of their children to be Christians is the highest service that parents can render to God. It is a work that demands patient labor, a lifelong diligent and persevering effort. By a neglect of this trust we prove ourselves unfaithful stewards. No excuse for such neglect will be accepted by God.

But those who have been guilty of neglect are not to despair. The woman whose coin was lost searched until she found it. So in love, faith, and prayer let parents work for their households, until with joy they can come to God saying, "Behold, I and the children whom the Lord hath given me." Isaiah 8:18.

This is true home missionary work, and it is as helpful to those who do it as to those for whom it is done. By our faithful interest for the home circle we are fitting ourselves to work for the members of the Lord's family, with whom, if loyal to Christ, we shall live through eternal ages. For our brethren and sisters in Christ we are to show the same interest that as members of one family we have for one another.

And God designs that all this shall fit us to labor for still others. As our sympathies shall broaden and our love increase, we shall find everywhere a work to do. God's great human household embraces the world, and none of its members are to be passed by with neglect.

Wherever we may be, there the lost piece of silver awaits our search. Are we seeking for it? Day by day we meet with those who take no interest in religious things; we talk with them, we visit among them; do we show an interest in their spiritual welfare? Do we present Christ to them as the sin-pardoning Saviour? With our own hearts warm with the love of Christ, do we tell them about that love? If we do not, how shall we meet these souls—lost, eternally lost—when with them we stand before the throne of God?

The value of a soul, who can estimate? Would you know its worth, go to Gethsemane, and there watch with Christ through those hours of anguish, when He sweat as it were great drops of blood. Look upon the Saviour uplifted on the cross. Hear the despairing cry, "My God, My God, why hast Thou forsaken Me?" Mark 15:34. Look upon the wounded head, the pierced side, the marred feet. Remember that Christ risked all. For our redemption heaven itself was imperiled. At the foot of the cross, remembering that for one sin-

The greater their sin and the deeper their misery, the more earnest and tender will be your efforts for their recovery.

ner Christ would have laid down His life, you may estimate the value of a soul.

If you are in communion with Christ, you will place His estimate upon every human being. You will feel for others the same deep love that Christ has felt for you. Then you will be able to win, not drive, to attract, not repulse, those for whom He died. None would ever have been brought back to God if Christ had not made a personal effort for them, and it is by this personal work that we can rescue souls. When you see those who are going down to death, you will not rest in quiet indifference and ease. The greater their sin and the deeper their misery, the more earnest and tender will be your efforts for their recovery. You will discern the need of those who are suffering, who have been sinning against God, and who are oppressed with a burden of guilt. Your heart will go out in sympathy for them, and you will reach out to them a helping hand. In the arms of your faith and love you will bring them to Christ. You will watch over and encourage them, and your sympathy and confidence will make it hard for them to fall from their steadfastness.

In this work all the angels of heaven are ready to cooperate. All the resources of heaven are at the command of those who are seeking to save the lost. Angels will help you to reach the most careless and the most hardened. And when one is brought back to God, all heaven is made glad; seraphs and cherubs touch their golden harps and sing praises to God and the Lamb for their mercy and loving-kindness to the children of men.

HTL-5

"The goodness of God leadeth thee to repentance" (Rom. 2:4).

Based on Luke 15:11-32

The Runaway

The parables of the lost coin, and the prodigal son, bring out in distinct lines God's pitying love for those who are straying from Him. Although they have turned away from God, He does not leave them in their misery. He is full of kindness and tender pity toward all who are exposed to the temptations of the artful foe.

In the parable of the prodigal son is presented the Lord's dealing with those who have once known the Father's love, but who have allowed the tempter to lead them captive at his will.

"A certain man had two sons: and the younger of them said to his father, Father, give me the portion of goods that falleth to me. And he divided unto them his living. And not many days after the younger son gathered all together, and took his journey into a far country."

This younger son had become weary of the restraint of his father's house. He thought that his liberty was restricted. His father's love and care for him were misinterpreted, and he determined to follow the dictates of his own inclination.

The youth acknowledges no obligation to his father, and expresses no gratitude; yet he claims the privilege of a child in sharing his father's goods. The inheritance that would fall to him at his father's death he desires to receive now. He is bent on present enjoyment, and cares not for the future.

Having obtained his patrimony, he goes into "a far country," away from his father's home. With money in plenty and liberty to do as he likes, he flatters himself that the desire of his heart is reached. There is no one to say, Do not do this, for it will be an injury to yourself; or, Do this, because it is right. Evil companions help him to plunge ever deeper into sin, and he wastes his "substance with riotous living."

The Bible tells of men who "professing themselves to be wise . . . became fools" (Romans 1:22); and this is the history of the young man of the parable. The wealth which he has selfishly claimed from his father he squanders upon harlots. The treasure of his young manhood is wasted. The precious years of life, the strength of intellect, the bright visions of youth, the spiritual aspirations—all are consumed in the fires of lust.

A great famine arises, he begins to be in want, and he joins himself to a citizen of the country, who sends him into the field to feed swine. To a Jew this was the most menial and degrading of employments. The youth who has boasted of his liberty now finds himself a slave. He is in the worst of bondage—"holden with the cords of his sins." Proverbs 5:22. The glitter and tinsel that enticed him have disappeared, and he feels the burden of his chain. Sitting upon the ground in that desolate and famine-stricken land, with no companions but the swine, he is fain to fill himself with the husks on which the beasts are fed. Of the gay companions who flocked about him in his prosperous days and ate and drank at his expense, there is not one left to befriend him. Where now is his riotous joy? Stilling his conscience, benumbing his sensibilities, he thought himself happy; but now, with money spent, with hunger unsatisfied, with pride humbled, with his moral nature dwarfed, with his will weak and untrustworthy, with his finer feelings seemingly dead, he is the most wretched of mortals.

Whatever the appearance may be, every life centered in self is squandered.

What a picture here of the sinner's state! Although surrounded with the blessings of His love, there is nothing that the sinner, bent on self-indulgence and sinful pleasure, desires so much as separation from God. Like the ungrateful son, he claims the good things of God as his by right. He takes them as a matter of course, and makes no return of gratitude, renders no service of love. As Cain went out from the presence of the Lord to seek his home; as the prodigal wandered into the "far country," so do sinners seek happiness in forgetfulness of God. (Romans 1:28.)

Whatever the appearance may be, every life centered in self is squandered. Whoever attempts to live apart from God is wasting his substance. He is squandering the precious years, squandering the powers of mind and heart and soul, and working to make himself bankrupt for eternity. The man who separates from God that he may serve himself, is the slave of mammon. The mind that God created for the companionship of angels has become degraded to the service of that which is earthly and bestial. This is the end to which self-serving tends.

If you have chosen such a life, you know that you are spending money for that which is not bread, and labor for that which satisfieth not. There come to you hours when you realize your degradation. Alone in the far country you feel your misery, and in despair you cry, "O wretched man that I am! who shall deliver me from the body of this death?" Romans 7:24. It is the statement of a universal truth which is contained in the prophet's words, "Cursed be the man that trusteth in man, and maketh flesh his arm, and whose heart departeth from the Lord. For he shall be like the heath in the desert, and shall not see when good cometh; but shall inhabit the parched places in the wilderness, in a salt land and not inhabited." Jeremiah 17:5, 6. God "maketh His sun to rise on the evil and on the good, and sendeth rain on the just and on the unjust" (Matthew 5:45); but men have the power to shut themselves away from sunshine and shower. So while the Sun of Righteousness shines, and the showers of grace fall freely for all, we may by separating ourselves from God still "inhabit the parched places in the wilderness."

The love of God still yearns over the one who has chosen to separate from Him, and He sets in operation influences to bring him back to the Father's house. The prodigal son in his wretchedness "came to himself." The deceptive power that Satan had exercised over him was broken. He saw that his suffering was the result of his own folly, and he said, "How many hired servants of my father's have bread enough and to spare, and I perish with hunger! I will arise and go to my father." Miserable as he was, the prodigal found hope in the conviction of his father's love. It was that love which was drawing him toward home. So it is the assurance of God's love that constrains the sinner to return to God. "The goodness of God leadeth thee to repentance." Romans 2:4. A golden chain, the mercy and compassion of divine love, is passed around every imperiled soul. The Lord declared, "I have loved thee with an everlasting love: therefore with lovingkindness have I drawn thee." Jeremiah 31:3.

The son determines to confess his guilt. He will go to his father, saying, "I have sinned against heaven, and before thee, and am no more worthy to be called thy son." But he adds, showing how stinted is his conception of his father's love, "Make me as one of thy hired servants."

The young man turns from the swineherds and the husks, and sets his face toward home. Trembling with weakness and faint from hunger, he presses eagerly on his way. He has no covering to conceal his rags; but his misery has conquered pride, and he hurries on to beg a servant's place where he was once a child.

Little did the gay, thoughtless youth, as he went out from his father's gate, dream of the ache and longing left in that father's heart. When he danced and feasted with his wild companions, little did he think of the shadow that had fallen on his home. And now as with weary and painful steps he pursues the homeward way, he knows not that one is watching for his return. But while he is yet "a great way off" the father discerns his form. Love is of quick sight. Not even the degradation of the years of sin can conceal the son from the father's eyes. He "had compassion, and ran, and fell on his neck" in a long, clinging, tender embrace.

A golden chain, the mercy and compassion of divine love, is passed around every imperiled soul.

The father will permit no contemptuous eye to mock at his son's misery and tatters. He takes from his own shoulders the broad, rich mantle, and wraps it around the son's wasted form, and the youth sobs out his repentance, saying, "Father, I have sinned against heaven, and in thy sight, and am no more worthy to be called thy son." The father holds him close to his side, and brings him home. No opportunity is given him to ask a servant's place. He is a son, who shall be honored with the best the house affords, and whom the waiting men and women shall respect and serve.

The father said to his servants, "Bring forth

the best robe, and put it on him; and put a ring on his hand, and shoes on his feet: and bring hither the fatted calf, and kill it; and let us eat, and be merry: for this my son was dead, and is alive again; he was lost, and is found. And they began to be merry."

In his restless youth the prodigal looked upon his father as stern and severe. How different his conception of him now! So those who are deceived by Satan look upon God as hard and exacting. They regard Him as watching to denounce and condemn, as unwilling to receive the sinner so long as there is a legal excuse for not helping him. His law they regard as a restriction upon men's happiness, a burdensome yoke from which they are glad to escape. But he whose eyes have been opened by the love of Christ will behold God as full of compassion. He does not appear as a tyrannical, relentless being, but as a father longing to embrace his repenting son. The sinner will exclaim with the psalmist, "Like as a father pitieth his children, so the Lord pitieth them that fear Him." Psalm 103:13.

Do not listen to the enemy's suggestion to stay away from Christ . . . until you are good enough to come to God.

In the parable there is no taunting, no casting up to the prodigal of his evil course. The son feels that the past is forgiven and forgotten, blotted out forever. And so God says to the sinner, "I have blotted out, as a thick cloud, thy transgressions, and, as a cloud, thy sins." Isaiah 44:22. "I will forgive their iniquity, and I will remember their sin no more." Jeremiah 31:34. "Let the wicked forsake his way, and the unrighteous man his thoughts: and let him return unto the Lord, and He will have mercy upon him; and to our God, for He will abundantly pardon." Isaiah 55:7. "In those days, and in that time, saith the Lord, the iniquity of Israel shall be sought for, and there shall be none; and the sins of Judah, and they shall not be found." Jeremiah 50:20.

What assurance here of God's willingness to receive the repenting sinner! Have you, reader, chosen your own way? Have you wandered far from God? Have you sought to feast upon the fruits of transgression, only to find them turn to ashes upon your lips? And now, your substance spent, your life-plans thwarted, and your hopes dead, do you sit alone and desolate? Now that voice which has long been speaking to your heart but to which you would not listen comes to you distinct and clear: "Arise ye, and depart; for this is not your rest: because it is polluted, it shall destroy you, even with a sore destruction." Micah 2:10. Return to your Father's house. He invites you, saying, "Return unto Me; for I have redeemed thee." Isaiah 44:22.

Do not listen to the enemy's suggestion to stay away from Christ until you have made yourself better; until you are good enough to come to God. If you wait until then, you will never come. When Satan points to your filthy garments, repeat the promise of Jesus, "Him that cometh to Me I will in no wise cast out." John 6:37. Tell the enemy that the blood of Jesus Christ cleanses from all sin. Make the prayer of David your own, "Purge me with hyssop, and I shall be clean: wash me, and I shall be whiter than snow." Psalm 51:7.

Arise and go to your Father. He will meet you a great way off. If you take even one step toward Him in repentance, He will hasten to enfold you in His arms of infinite love. His ear is open to the cry of the contrite soul. The very first reaching out of the heart after God is known to Him. Never a prayer is offered, however faltering, never a tear is shed, however secret, never a sincere desire after God is cherished, however feeble, but the Spirit of God goes forth to meet it. Even before the prayer is uttered or the yearning of the heart made known, grace from Christ goes forth to meet the grace that is working upon the human soul.

Your heavenly Father will take from you the garments defiled by sin. In the beautiful parabolic prophecy of Zechariah, the high priest Joshua, standing clothed in filthy garments before the angel of the Lord, represents the sinner. And the word is spoken by the Lord, "Take away the filthy garments from him. And unto him He said, Behold, I have caused thine iniquity to pass from thee, and I will clothe thee with change of raiment. . . . So they set a fair mitre upon his head, and clothed him with garments." Zechariah 3:4, 5. Even so God will clothe you with "the garments of salvation," and cover you with "the robe of righteousness." Isaiah 61:10. "Though ye have lien among the pots, yet shall ye be as the wings of a dove covered with silver, and her feathers with yellow gold." Psalm 68:13.

He will bring you into His banqueting house, and His banner over you shall be love. (Canticles 2:4.) "If thou wilt walk in My ways," He declares, "I will give thee places to walk among these that stand by"—even among the holy angels that surround His throne. (Zechariah 3:7.)

"As the bridegroom rejoiceth over the bride, so shall thy God rejoice over thee." Isaiah 62:5. "He will save, He will rejoice over thee with joy; He will rest in His love, He will joy over thee with singing." Zephaniah 3:17. And heaven and earth shall unite in the Father's song of rejoicing: "For this My son was dead, and is alive again; he was lost, and is found."

Thus far in the Saviour's parable there is no discordant note to jar the harmony of the scene of joy; but now Christ introduces another element. When the prodigal came home the elder son "was in the field: and as he came and drew nigh to the house, he heard music and dancing. And he called one of the servants, and asked what these things meant. And he said unto him, Thy brother is come; and thy father hath killed the fatted calf, because he hath received him safe and sound. And he was angry, and would not go in." This elder brother has not been sharing in his father's anxiety and watching for the one that was lost. He shares not, therefore, in the father's joy at the wanderer's return. The sounds of rejoicing kindle no gladness in his heart. He inquires of a servant the reason of the festivity, and the answer excites his jealousy. He will not go in to welcome his lost brother. The favor shown the prodigal he regards as an insult to himself.

Never a prayer is offered, however faltering, never a tear is shed, . . . but the Spirit of God goes forth to meet it.

When the father comes out to remonstrate with him, the pride and malignity of his nature are revealed. He dwells upon his own life in his father's house as a round of unrequited service, and then places in mean contrast the favor shown to the son just returned. He makes it plain that his own service has been that of a servant rather than a son. When he should have found an abiding joy in his father's presence, his mind has rested upon the profit to accrue from his circumspect life. His words show that it is for this he has forgone the pleasures of sin. Now if this brother is to share in the father's gifts, the elder son counts that he himself has been wronged. He grudges his brother the favor shown him. He plainly shows that had he been in the father's place, he would not have received the prodigal. He does not even acknowledge him as a brother, but coldly speaks of him as "thy son."

When you see yourselves as sinners saved only by the love of your heavenly Father, you will have tender pity for others who are suffering.

Yet the father deals tenderly with him. "Son," he says, "thou art ever with me, and all that I have is thine." Through all these years of your brother's outcast life, have you not had the privilege of companionship with me?

Everything that could minister to the happiness of his children was freely theirs. The son need have no question of gift or reward. "All that I have is thine." You have only to believe my love, and take the gift that is freely bestowed.

One son had for a time cut himself off from the household, not discerning the father's love. But now he had returned, and the tide of joy sweeps away every disturbing thought. "This thy brother was dead, and is alive again; and was lost, and is found."

Was the elder brother brought to see his own mean, ungrateful spirit? Did he come to see that though his brother had done wickedly, he was his brother still? Did the elder brother repent of his jealousy and hardheartedness? Concerning this Christ was silent. For the parable was still enacting, and it rested with His hearers to determine what the outcome should be.

By the elder son were represented the unrepenting Jews of Christ's day, and also the Pharisees in every age, who look with contempt upon those whom they regard as publicans and sinners. Because they themselves have not gone to great excesses in vice, they are filled with self-righteousness. Christ met these cavilers on their own ground. Like the elder son in the parable, they had enjoyed special privileges from God. They claimed to be sons in God's house, but they had the spirit of the hireling. They were working, not from love, but from hope of reward. In their eyes God was an exacting taskmaster. They saw Christ inviting publicans and sinners to receive freely the gift of His grace—the gift which the rabbis hoped to secure only by toil and penance—and they were offended. The prodigal's return, which filled the Father's heart with joy, only stirred them to jealousy.

In the parable the father's remonstrance with the elder son was Heaven's tender appeal to the Pharisees. "All that I have is thine"—not as wages, but as a gift. Like the prodigal, you can receive it only as the unmerited bestowal of the Father's love.

Self-righteousness not only leads men to misrepresent God, but makes them cold-hearted and critical toward their brethren. The elder son, in his selfishness and jealousy, stood ready to watch his brother, to criticize every action, and to accuse him for the least deficiency. He would detect every mistake, and make the most of every wrong act. Thus he would seek to justify his own unforgiving spirit. Many today are doing the same thing. While the soul is making its very first struggles against a flood of temptations, they stand by, stubborn, self-willed, complaining, accusing. They may claim to be children of God, but they are acting out the spirit of Satan. By their attitude toward their brethren these accusers place themselves where God cannot give them the light of His countenance.

Many are constantly questioning, "Wherewith shall I come before the Lord, and bow myself before the high God? Shall I come before Him with burnt offerings, with calves of a year old? Will the Lord be pleased with thousands of rams, or with ten thousands of rivers of oil?" But "He hath shewed thee, O man, what is good; and what doth the Lord require of thee, but to do justly, and to love mercy, and to walk humbly with thy God?" Micah 6:6-8.

This is the service that God has chosen—"to loose the bands of wickedness, to undo the heavy burdens, and to let the oppressed go free, and that ye break every yoke, . . . and that thou hide not thyself from thine own flesh." Isaiah 58:6, 7. When you see yourselves as sinners saved only by the love of your heavenly Father, you will have tender pity for others who are suffering in sin. You will no longer meet misery and repentance with jealousy and censure. When the ice of selfishness is melted from your hearts, you will be in sympathy with God, and will share His joy in the saving of the lost.

It is true that you claim to be a child of God; but if this claim be true, it is "thy brother" that was "dead, and is alive again; and was lost, and is found." He is bound to you by the closest ties, for God recognizes him as a son. Deny your relationship to him, and you show that you are but a hireling in the household, not a child in the family of God.

Though you will not join in the greeting to the lost, the joy will go on, the restored one will have his place by the Father's side and in the Father's work. He that is forgiven much, the same loves much. But you will be in the darkness without. For "he that loveth not knoweth not God; for God is love." 1 John 4:8.

"Thou shalt love the Lord thy God with all thine heart, and with all thy soul, and all thy might" (Deut. 6:5).

Based on Luke 16:19-31

In the parable of the rich man and Lazarus, Christ shows that in this life men decide their eternal destiny. During probationary time the grace of God is offered to every soul. But if men waste their opportunities in self-pleasing, they cut themselves off from everlasting life. No afterprobation will be granted them. By their own choice they have fixed an impassable gulf between them and their God.

This parable draws a contrast between the rich who have not made God their dependence, and the poor who have made God their dependence. Christ shows that the time is coming when the position of the two classes will be reversed. Those who are poor in this world's goods, yet who trust in God and are patient in suffering, will one day be exalted above those who now hold the highest positions the world can give but who have not surrendered their life to God.

"There was a certain rich man," Christ said, "which was clothed in purple and fine linen, and fared sumptuously every day. And there was a certain beggar named Lazarus, which was laid at his gate, full of sores, and desiring to be fed with the crumbs which fell from the rich man's table."

The rich man did not belong to the class represented by the unjust judge, who openly declared his disregard for God and man. He claimed to be a son of Abraham. He did not treat the beggar with violence or require him to go away because the sight of him was disagreeable. If the poor, loathsome specimen of humanity could be comforted by beholding him as he entered his gates, the rich man was willing that he should remain. But he was selfishly indifferent to the needs of his suffering brother.

There were then no hospitals in which the sick might be cared for. The suffering and needy were brought to the notice of those to whom the Lord had entrusted wealth, that they might receive help and sympathy. Thus it was with the beggar and the rich man. Lazarus was in great need of help; for he was without friends, home, money, or food. Yet he was allowed to remain in this condition day after day, while the wealthy nobleman had every want supplied. The one who was abundantly able to relieve the sufferings of his fellow creature, lived to himself, as many live today.

There are today close beside us many who are hungry, naked, and homeless. A neglect to impart of our means to these needy, suffering ones places upon us a burden of guilt which we shall one day fear to meet. All covetousness is condemned as idolatry. All selfish indulgence is an offense in God's sight.

God had made the rich man a steward of His means, and it was his duty to attend to just such cases as that of the beggar. The command had been given. "Thou shalt love the Lord thy God with all thine heart, and with all thy soul, and with all thy might" (Deuteronomy 6:5); and "thou shalt love thy neighbour as thyself" (Leviticus 19:18). The rich man was a Jew, and he was acquainted with the command of God. But he forgot that he was accountable for the use of his entrusted means and capabilities. The Lord's blessings rested upon him abundantly, but he employed them selfishly, to honor himself, not his Maker. In proportion to his abundance was his obligation to use his gifts for the uplifting of humanity. This was the Lord's command, but the rich man had no thought of his obligation to God. He lent money, and took interest for what he loaned; but he returned no interest for what God had lent him. He had knowledge and talents, but did not improve them. Forgetful of his accountability to God, he devoted all his powers to pleasure. Everything with which he was surrounded, his round of amusements, the praise and flattery of his friends, ministered to his selfish enjoyment. So engrossed was he in the society of his friends that he lost all sense of his responsibility to co-operate with God in His ministry of mercy. He had opportunity to understand the word of God, and to practice its teachings; but the pleasure-loving society he chose so occupied his time that he forgot the God of eternity.

There are today close beside us many who are hungry, naked, and homeless.

The time came when a change took place in the condition of the two men. The poor man had suffered day by day, but he had patiently and quietly endured. In the course of time he died and was buried. There was no one to mourn for him; but by his patience in suffering he had witnessed for Christ, he had endured the test of his faith, and at his death he is represented as being carried by the angels into Abraham's bosom.

Lazarus represents the suffering poor who believe in Christ. When the trumpet sounds and all that are in the graves hear Christ's voice and come forth, they will receive their reward; for their faith in God was not a mere theory but a reality.

"The rich man also died, and was buried; and in hell he lift up his eyes, being in torments, and seeth Abraham afar off, and Lazarus in his bosom. And he cried and said, Father Abraham, have mercy on me, and send Lazarus, that he may dip the tip of his finger in water, and cool my tongue; for I am tormented in this flame."

In this parable Christ was meeting the people on their own ground. The doctrine of a conscious state of existence between death and the resurrection was held by many of those who were listening to Christ's words. The Saviour knew of their ideas, and He framed His parable so as to inculcate important truths through these preconceived opinions. He held up before His hearers a mirror wherein they might see themselves in their true relation to God. He used the prevailing opinion to convey the idea He wished to make prominent to all—that no man is valued for his possessions; for all he has belongs to him only as lent by the Lord. A misuse of these gifts will place him below the poorest and most afflicted man who loves God and trusts in Him.

Christ desires His hearers to understand that it is impossible for men to secure the salvation of the soul after death. "Son," Abraham is represented as answering, "remember that thou in thy lifetime receivedst thy good things, and likewise Lazarus evil things: but now he is comforted, and thou art tormented. And beside all this, between us and you there is a great gulf fixed: so that they which would pass from hence to you cannot; neither can they pass to us, that would come from thence." Thus Christ represented the hopelessness of looking for a second probation. This life is the only time given to man in which to prepare for eternity.

The rich man had not abandoned the idea that he was a child of Abraham, and in his distress he is represented as calling upon him for aid. "Father Abraham," he prayed, "have mercy on me." He did not pray to God but to Abraham. Thus he showed that he placed Abraham above God, and that he relied on his relationship to Abraham for salvation. The thief on the cross offered his prayer to Christ. "Remember me when Thou comest into Thy kingdom," he said. (Luke 23:42.) And at once the response came, Verily I say unto thee today (as I hang on the cross in humiliation and suffering), thou shalt be with Me in Paradise. But the rich man prayed to Abraham, and his petition was not granted. Christ alone is exalted to be "a Prince and a Saviour, for to give repentance to Israel, and forgiveness of sins." Acts 5:31. "Neither is there salvation in any other." Acts 4:12.

The rich man had spent his life in self-pleasing, and too late he saw that he had made no provision for eternity. He realized his folly, and thought of his brothers, who would go on as he had gone, living to please themselves. Then he made the request, "I pray thee therefore, father, that thou wouldest send him [Lazarus] to my father's house: for I have five brethren; that he may testify unto them, lest they also come into this place of torment." But "Abraham saith unto him, They have Moses and the prophets; let them hear them. And he said, Nay, father Abraham: but if one went unto them from the dead, they will repent. And he said unto him, If they hear not Moses and the prophets, neither will they be persuaded, though one rose from the dead."

Christ desires His hearers to understand that it is impossible . . . to secure the salvation of the soul after death.

When the rich man solicited additional evidence for his brothers, he was plainly told that should this evidence be given, they would not be persuaded. His request cast a reflection on God.

It was as if the rich man had said, If you had more thoroughly warned me, I should not now be here. Abraham, in his answer to this request, is represented as saying, Your brothers have been sufficiently warned. Light has been given them, but they would not see; truth has been presented to them, but they would not hear.

"If they hear not Moses and the prophets, neither will they be persuaded, though one rose from the dead." These words were proved true in the history of the Jewish nation. Christ's last and crowning miracle was the raising of Lazarus of Bethany, after he had been dead four days.

God gives to everyone sufficient light and grace to do the work He has given him to do.

The Jews were given this wonderful evidence of the Saviour's divinity, but they rejected it. Lazarus rose from the dead and bore his testimony before them, but they hardened their hearts against all evidence, and even sought to take his life. (John 12:9-11).

The law and prophets are God's appointed agencies for the salvation of men. Christ said, Let them give heed to these evidences. If they do not listen to the voice of God in His word, the testimony of a witness raised from the dead would not be heeded.

Those who heed Moses and the prophets will require no greater light than God has given; but if men reject the light, and fail to appreciate the opportunities granted them, they would not hear if one from the dead should come to them with a message. They would not be convinced even by this evidence; for those who reject the law and the prophets so harden their hearts that they will reject all light.

The conversation between Abraham and the once-rich man is figurative. The lesson to be gathered from it is that every man is given sufficient light for the discharge of the duties required of him. Man's responsibilities are proportionate to his opportunities and privileges. God gives to everyone sufficient light and grace to do the work He has given him to do. If man fails to do that which a little light shows to be his duty, greater light would only reveal unfaithfulness, neglect to improve the blessings given. "He that is faithful in that which is least is faithful also in much: and he that is unjust in the least is unjust also in much." Luke 16:10. Those who refuse to be enlightened by Moses and the prophets and ask for some wonderful miracle to be performed would not be convinced if their wish were granted.

The parable of the rich man and Lazarus shows how the two classes represented by these men are estimated in the unseen world. There is no sin in being rich if riches are not acquired by injustice. A rich man is not condemned for having riches, but condemnation rests upon him if the means entrusted to him is spent in selfishness. Far better might he lay up his money beside the throne of God, by using it to do good. Death cannot make any man poor who thus devotes himself to seeking eternal riches. But the man who hoards his treasure for self cannot take any of it to heaven. He has proved himself to be an unfaithful steward. During his lifetime he had his good things, but he was forgetful of his obligation to God. He failed of securing the heavenly treasure.

The rich man who had so many privileges is represented to us as one who should have cultivated his gifts, so that his works should reach to the great beyond, carrying with them improved spiritual advantages. It is the purpose of redemption, not only to blot out sin, but to give back to man those spiritual gifts lost because of sin's dwarfing power. Money cannot be carried into the next life; it is not needed there; but the good deeds done in winning souls to Christ are carried to the heavenly courts. But those who selfishly spend the Lord's gifts on themselves, leaving their needy fellow creatures without aid and doing nothing to advance God's work in the world, dishonor their Maker. Robbery of God is written opposite their names in the books of heaven.

The rich man had all that money could procure, but he did not possess the riches that would have kept his account right with God. He had lived as if all that he possessed were his own. He had neglected the call of God and the claims of the suffering poor. But at length there comes a call which he cannot neglect. By a power which he cannot question or resist he is commanded to quit the premises of which he is no longer steward. The once-rich man is reduced to hopeless poverty. The robe of Christ's righteousness, woven in the loom of heaven, can never cover him. He who once wore the richest purple, the finest linen, is reduced to nakedness. His probation is ended. He brought nothing into the world, and he can take nothing out of it.

Christ lifted the curtain and presented this picture before priests and rulers, scribes and Pharisees. Look at it, you who are rich in this world's goods and are not rich toward God. Will you not contemplate this scene? That which is highly esteemed among men is abhorrent in the sight of God. Christ asks, "What shall it profit a man, if he shall gain the whole world, and lose his own soul? or what shall a man give in exchange for his soul?" Mark 8:36, 37.

Application to the Jewish Nation

When Christ gave the parable of the rich man and Lazarus, there were many in the Jewish nation in the pitiable condition of the rich man, using the Lord's goods for selfish gratification, preparing themselves to hear the sentence, "Thou art weighed in the balances, and art found wanting." Daniel 5:27. The rich man was favored with every temporal and spiritual blessing, but he refused to cooperate with God in the use of these blessings. Thus it was with the Jewish nation. The Lord had made the Jews the depositaries of sacred truth. He had appointed them stewards of His grace. He had given them every spiritual and temporal advantage, and He called upon them to impart these blessings. Special instruction had been given them in regard to their treatment of their brethren who had fallen into decay, of the stranger within their gates, and of the poor among them. They were not to seek to gain everything for their own advantage, but were to remember those in need

They were not to seek to gain everything for their own advantage, but were to remember those in need and share with them.

and share with them. And God promised to bless them in accordance with their deeds of love and mercy. But like the rich man, they put forth no helping hand to relieve the temporal or spiritual necessities of suffering humanity. Filled with pride, they regarded themselves as the chosen and favored people of God; yet they did not serve or worship God. They put their dependence in the fact that they were children of Abraham. "We be Abraham's seed," they said proudly. (John 8:33.) When the crisis came, it was revealed that they had divorced themselves from God, and had placed their trust in Abraham, as if he were God.

The soul that longs after the excitement of worldly pleasure, the mind that is full of love for display, cannot serve God.

Christ longed to let light shine into the darkened minds of the Jewish people. He said to them, "If ye were Abraham's children, ye would do the works of Abraham. But now ye seek to kill Me, a man that hath told you the truth, which I have heard of God: this did not Abraham." John 8:39, 40.

Christ recognized no virtue in lineage. He taught that spiritual connection supersedes all natural connection. The Jews claimed to have descended from Abraham; but by failing to do the works of Abraham, they proved that they were not his true children. Only those who prove themselves to be spiritually in harmony with Abraham by obeying the voice of God, are reckoned as of true descent. Although the beggar belonged to the class looked upon by men as inferior, Christ recognized him as one whom Abraham would take into the very closest friendship.

The rich man, though surrounded with all the luxuries of life, was so ignorant that he put Abraham where God should have been. If he had appreciated his exalted privileges and had allowed God's Spirit to mold his mind and heart, he would have had an altogether different position. So with the nation he represented. If they had responded to the divine call, their future would have been wholly different. They would have shown true spiritual discernment. They had means which God would have increased, making it sufficient to bless and enlighten the whole world. But they had so far separated from the Lord's arrangement that their whole life was perverted. They failed to use their gifts as God's stewards in accordance with truth and righteousness. Eternity was not brought into their reckoning, and the result of their unfaithfulness was ruin to the whole nation.

Christ knew that at the destruction of Jerusalem the Jews would remember His warning. And it was so. When calamity came upon Jerusalem, when starvation and suffering of every kind came upon the people, they remembered these words of Christ and understood the parable. They had brought their suffering upon themselves by their neglect to let their God-given light shine forth to the world.

The closing scenes of this earth's history are portrayed in the closing of the rich man's history. The rich man claimed to be a son of Abraham, but he was separated from Abraham

by an impassable gulf—a character wrongly developed. Abraham served God, following His word in faith and obedience. But the rich man was unmindful of God and of the needs of suffering humanity. The great gulf fixed between him and Abraham was the gulf of disobedience. There are many today who are following the same course. Though church members, they are unconverted. They may take part in the church service; they may chant the psalm, "As the hart panteth after the water brooks, so panteth my soul after Thee, O God" (Psalm 42:1); but they testify to a falsehood. They are no more righteous in God's sight than is the veriest sinner. The soul that longs after the excitement of worldly pleasure, the mind that is full of love for display, cannot serve God. Like the rich man in the parable, such a one has no inclination to war against the lust of the flesh. He longs to indulge appetite. He chooses the atmosphere of sin. He is suddenly snatched away by death, and he goes down to the grave with the character formed during his lifetime in copartnership with satanic agencies. In the grave he has no power to choose anything, be it good or evil; for in the day when a man dies, his thoughts perish. (Psalm 146:4; Ecclesiastes 9:5, 6.)

When the voice of God awakes the dead he will come from the grave with the same appetites and passions, the same likes and dislikes, that he cherished when living. God works no miracle to re-create a man who would not be re-created when he was granted every opportunity and provided with every facility. During his lifetime he took no delight in God, nor found pleasure in His service. His character is not in harmony with God, and he could not be happy in the heavenly family.

Today there is a class in our world who are self-righteous. They are not gluttons, they are not drunkards, they are not infidels; but they desire to live for themselves, not for God. He is not in their thoughts; therefore they are classed with unbelievers. Were it possible for them to enter the gates of the city of God, they could have no right to the tree of life, for when God's commandments were laid before them with all their binding claims they said, No. They have not served God here; therefore they would not serve Him hereafter. They could not live in His presence, and they would feel that any place was preferable to heaven.

To learn of Christ means to receive His grace, which is His character. But those who do not appreciate and utilize the precious opportunities and sacred influences granted them on earth, are not fitted to take part in the pure devotion of heaven. Their characters are not molded according to the divine similitude. By their own neglect they have formed a chasm which nothing can bridge. Between them and the righteous there is a great gulf fixed.

"Buy of Me . . . raiment, that thou mayest be clothed" (Rev. 3:18).

Based on Matthew 22:1-14

THE WEDDING GARMENT

The parable of the wedding garment opens before us a lesson of the highest consequence. By the marriage is represented the union of humanity with divinity; the wedding garment represents the character which all must possess who shall be accounted fit guests for the wedding.

In this parable, as in that of the great supper, are illustrated the gospel invitation, its rejection by the Jewish people, and the call of mercy to the Gentiles. But on the part of those who reject the invitation, this parable brings to view a deeper insult and a more dreadful punishment. The call to the feast is a king's invitation. It proceeds from one who is vested with power to command. It confers high honor. Yet the honor is unappreciated. The king's authority is despised. While the householder's invitation was regarded with indifference, the king's is met with insult and murder. They treated his servants with scorn, despitefully using them and slaying them.

The householder, on seeing his invitation slighted, declared that none of the men who were bidden should taste of his supper. But for those who had done despite to the king, more than exclusion from his presence and his table is decreed. "He sent forth his armies, and destroyed those murderers, and burned up their city."

In both parables the feast is provided with guests, but the second shows that there is a preparation to be made by all who attend the feast. Those who neglect this preparation are cast out. "The king came in to see the guests," and "saw there a man which had not on a wedding garment; and he saith unto him, Friend, how camest thou in hither not having a wedding garment? And he was speechless. Then said the king to the servants, Bind him hand and foot, and take him away, and cast him into outer darkness; there shall be weeping and gnashing of teeth."

The call to the feast had been given by Christ's disciples. Our Lord had sent out the twelve and afterward the seventy, proclaiming that the kingdom of God was at hand, and calling upon men to repent and believe the gospel. But the call was not heeded. Those who were bidden to the feast did not come. The servants were sent out later to say, "Behold, I have prepared my dinner; my oxen and my fatlings are killed, and all things are ready: come unto the marriage." This was the message borne to the Jewish nation after the crucifixion of Christ; but the nation that claimed to be God's peculiar people rejected the gospel brought to them in the power of the Holy Spirit. Many did this in the most scornful manner. Others were so exasperated by the offer of salvation, the offer of pardon for rejecting the Lord of glory, that they turned upon the bearers of the message. There

But not all who profess to be Christians are true disciples.

was "a great persecution." Acts 8:1. Many both of men and women were thrust into prison, and some of the Lord's messengers, as Stephen and James, were put to death.

Thus the Jewish people sealed their rejection of God's mercy. The result was foretold by Christ in the parable. The king "sent forth his armies, and destroyed those murderers, and burned up their city." The judgment pronounced came upon the Jews in the destruction of Jerusalem and the scattering of the nation.

The third call to the feast represents the giving of the gospel to the Gentiles. The king said, "The wedding is ready, but they which were bidden were not worthy. Go ye therefore into the highways, and as many as ye shall find, bid to the marriage."

The king's servants who went out into the highways "gathered together all as many as they found, both bad and good." It was a mixed company. Some of them had no more real regard for the giver of the feast than had the ones who rejected the call. The class first bidden could not afford, they thought, to sacrifice any worldly advantage for the sake of attending the king's banquet. And of those who accepted the invitation, there were some who thought only of benefiting themselves. They came to share the provisions of the feast, but had no desire to honor the king.

When the king came in to view the guests, the real character of all was revealed. For every guest at the feast there had been provided a wedding garment. This garment was a gift from the king. By wearing it the guests showed their respect for the giver of the feast. But one man was clothed in his common citizen dress. He had refused to make the preparation required by the king. The garment provided for him at great cost he disdained to wear. Thus he insulted his lord. To the king's demand, "How camest thou in hither not having a wedding garment?" he could answer nothing. He was self-condemned. Then the king said, "Bind him hand and foot, and take him away, and cast him into outer darkness."

By the king's examination of the guests at the feast is represented a work of judgment. The guests at the gospel feast are those who profess to serve God, those whose names are written in the book of life. But not all who profess to be Christians are true disciples. Before the final reward is given, it must be decided who are fitted to share the inheritance of the righteous. This decision must be made prior to the second coming of Christ in the clouds of heaven; for when He comes, His reward is with Him, "to give every man according as his work shall be." Revelation 22:12. Before His coming, then, the character of every man's work will have been determined, and to every one of Christ's followers the reward will have been apportioned according to his deeds.

It is while men are still dwelling upon the earth that the work of investigative judgment takes place in the courts of heaven. The lives of all His professed followers pass in review before God. All are examined according to the record of the books of heaven, and according to his deeds the destiny of each is forever fixed.

By the wedding garment in the parable is represented the pure, spotless character which Christ's true followers will possess. To the church it is given "that she should be arrayed in fine linen, clean and white," "not having spot, or wrinkle, or any such thing." Revelation 19:8. The fine linen, says the Scripture, "is the righteousness of saints." Ephesians 5:27. It is the righteousness of Christ, His own unblemished character, that through faith is imparted to all who receive Him as their personal Saviour.

The white robe of innocence was worn by our first parents when they were placed by God in holy Eden. They lived in perfect conformity to the will of God. All the strength of their affections was given to their heavenly Father. A beautiful soft light, the light of God, enshrouded the holy pair. This robe of light was a symbol of their spiritual garments of heavenly innocence. Had they remained true to God it would ever have continued to enshroud them. But when sin entered, they severed their connection with God, and the light that had encircled them departed. Naked and ashamed, they tried to supply the place of the heavenly garments by sewing together fig leaves for a covering.

This is what the transgressors of God's law have done ever since the day of Adam and Eve's disobedience. They have sewed together fig leaves to cover the nakedness caused by transgression. They have worn the garments of their own devising, by works of their own they have tried to cover their sins, and make themselves acceptable with God.

But this they can never do. Nothing can man devise to supply the place of his lost robe of innocence. No fig-leaf garment, no worldly citizen dress, can be worn by those who sit down with Christ and angels at the marriage supper of the Lamb.

Only the covering which Christ Himself has provided can make us meet to appear in God's presence. This covering, the robe of His own righteousness, Christ will put upon every repenting, believing soul. "I counsel thee," He

Only the covering which Christ Himself has provided can make us meet to appear in God's presence.

says, "to buy of Me . . . white raiment, that thou mayest be clothed, and that the shame of thy nakedness do not appear." Revelation 3:18.

This robe, woven in the loom of heaven, has in it not one thread of human devising. Christ in His humanity wrought out a perfect character, and this character He offers to impart to us. "All our righteousnesses are as filthy rags." Isaiah 64:6. Everything that we of ourselves can do is defiled by sin. But the Son of God "was manifested to take away our sins; and in Him is no sin." Sin is defined to be "the transgression of the law." 1 John 3:5, 4. But Christ was obedient to every requirement of the law. He said of Himself, "I delight to do Thy will, O My God; yea, Thy law is within My heart." Psalm 40:8. When on earth, He said to His disciples, "I have kept My Father's commandments." John 15:10. By His perfect obedience He has made it possible for every human being to obey God's commandments. When we submit ourselves to Christ, the heart is united with His heart, the will is merged in His will, the mind becomes one with His mind, the thoughts are brought into captivity to Him; we live His life. This is what it means to be clothed with the garment of His righteousness. Then as the Lord looks upon us He sees, not the fig-leaf garment, not the nakedness and deformity of sin, but His own robe of righteousness, which is perfect obedience to the law of Jehovah.

Our characters are revealed by what we do.

The guests at the marriage feast were inspected by the king. Only those were accepted who had obeyed his requirements and put on the wedding garment. So it is with the guests at the gospel feast. All must pass the scrutiny of the great King, and only those are received who have put on the robe of Christ's righteousness.

Righteousness is right doing, and it is by their deeds that all will be judged. Our characters are revealed by what we do. The works show whether the faith is genuine.

It is not enough for us to believe that Jesus is not an impostor, and that the religion of the Bible is no cunningly devised fable. We may believe that the name of Jesus is the only name under heaven whereby man may be saved, and yet we may not through faith make Him our personal Saviour. It is not enough to believe the theory of truth. It is not enough to make a profession of faith in Christ and have our names registered on the church roll. "He that keepeth His commandments dwelleth in Him, and He in him. And hereby we know that He abideth in us, by the Spirit which He hath given us." "Hereby we do know that we know Him if we keep His commandments." 1 John 3:24; 2:3. This is the genuine evidence of conversion. Whatever our profession, it amounts to nothing unless Christ is revealed in works of righteousness.

The truth is to be planted in the heart. It is to control the mind and regulate the affections. The whole character must be stamped with the divine utterances. Every jot and tittle of the word of God is to be brought into the daily practice.

He who becomes a partaker of the divine nature will be in harmony with God's great standard of righteousness, His holy law. This is the rule by which God measures the actions of men. This will be the test of character in the judgment.

There are many who claim that by the death of Christ the law was abrogated; but in this they contradict Christ's own words, "Think not that I am come to destroy the law, or the prophets.... Till heaven and earth pass, one jot or one tittle shall in no wise pass from the law." Matthew 5:17, 18. It was to atone for man's transgression of the law that Christ laid down His life. Could the law have been changed or set aside, then Christ need not have died. By His life on earth He honored the law of God. By His death He established it. He gave His life as a sacrifice, not to destroy God's law, not to create a lower standard, but that justice might be maintained, that the law might be shown to be immutable, that it might stand fast forever.

Satan had claimed that it was impossible for man to obey God's commandments; and in our own strength it is true that we cannot obey them. But Christ came in the form of humanity, and by His perfect obedience He proved that humanity and divinity combined can obey every one of God's precepts.

"As many as received Him, to them gave He power to become the sons of God, even to them that believe on His name." John 1:12. This power is not in the human agent. It is the power of God. When a soul receives Christ, he receives power to live the life of Christ.

God requires perfection of His children. His law is a transcript of His own character, and it is the standard of all character. This infinite standard is presented to all that there may be no mistake in regard to the kind of people whom God will have to compose His kingdom. The life of Christ on earth was a perfect expression of God's law, and when those who claim to be children of God become Christlike in character, they will be obedient to God's commandments. Then the Lord can trust them to be of the number who shall compose the family of heaven. Clothed in the glorious apparel of Christ's righteousness, they have a place at the King's feast. They have a right to join the blood-washed throng.

The man who came to the feast without a wedding garment represents the condition of many in our world today. They profess to be Christians, and lay claim to the blessings and privileges of the gospel; yet they feel no need of a transformation of character. They have never felt true repentance for sin. They do not realize their need of Christ or exercise faith in Him. They have not overcome their hereditary or cultivated tendencies to wrongdoing. Yet they think that they are good enough in themselves, and they rest upon their own merits instead of trusting in Christ. Hearers of the word, they come to the banquet, but they have not put on the robe of Christ's righteousness.

Many who call themselves Christians are mere human moralists. They have refused the gift which alone could enable them to honor Christ by representing Him to the world. The work of the Holy Spirit is to them a strange work. They are not doers of the word. The heavenly principles that distinguish those who are one with Christ from those who are one with the world have become almost indistinguishable. The professed followers of Christ are no longer a separate and peculiar people. The line

The life of Christ on earth was a perfect expression of God's law.

of demarcation is indistinct. The people are subordinating themselves to the world, to its practices, its customs, its selfishness. The church has gone over to the world in transgression of the law, when the world should have come over to the church in obedience to the law. Daily the church is being converted to the world.

All these expect to be saved by Christ's death, while they refuse to live His self-sacrificing life. They extol the riches of free grace, and attempt to cover themselves with an appearance of righteousness, hoping to screen their defects of character; but their efforts will be of no avail in the day of God.

The righteousness of Christ will not cover

one cherished sin. A man may be a law-breaker in heart; yet if he commits no outward act of transgression, he may be regarded by the world as possessing great integrity. But God's law looks into the secrets of the heart. Every act is judged by the motives that prompt it. Only that which is in accord with the principles of God's law will stand in the judgment.

God is love. He has shown that love in the gift of Christ. When "He gave His only begotten Son, that whosoever believeth in Him should not perish, but have everlasting life," He withheld nothing from His purchased possession (John 3:16). He gave all heaven, from which we may draw strength and efficiency, that we be not repulsed or overcome by our great adversary. But the love of God does not lead Him to excuse sin. He did not excuse it in Satan; He did not excuse it in Adam or in Cain; nor will He excuse it in any other of the children of men. He will not connive at our sins or overlook our defects of character. He expects us to overcome in His name.

The wedding garment, provided at infinite cost, is freely offered to every soul.

Those who reject the gift of Christ's righteousness are rejecting the attributes of character which would constitute them the sons and daughters of God. They are rejecting that which alone could give them a fitness for a place at the marriage feast.

In the parable, when the king inquired, "How camest thou in hither not having a wedding garment?" the man was speechless. So it will be in the great judgment day. Men may now excuse their defects of character, but in that day they will offer no excuse.

The professed churches of Christ in this generation are exalted to the highest privileges. The Lord has been revealed to us in ever-increasing light. Our privileges are far greater than were the privileges of God's ancient people. We have not only the great light committed to Israel, but we have the increased evidence of the great salvation brought to us through Christ. That which was type and symbol to the Jews is reality to us. They had the Old Testament history; we have that and the New Testament also. We have the assurance of a Saviour who has come, a Saviour who has been crucified, who has risen, and over the rent sepulcher of Joseph has proclaimed, "I am the resurrection and the life." In our knowledge of Christ and His love the kingdom of God is placed in the midst of us. Christ is revealed to us in sermons and chanted to us in songs. The spiritual banquet is set before us in rich abundance. The wedding garment, provided at infinite cost, is freely offered to every soul. By the messengers of God are presented to us the righteousness of Christ, justification by faith, the exceeding great and precious promises of God's word, free access to the Father by Christ, the comfort of the Spirit, the well-grounded assurance of eternal life in the kingdom of God. What could God do for us that He has not done in providing the great supper, the heavenly banquet?

In heaven it is said by the ministering angels: The ministry which we have been commissioned to perform we have done. We pressed back the army of evil angels. We sent brightness and light into the souls of men, quickening their memory of the love of God expressed in Jesus. We attracted their eyes to the cross of Christ. Their hearts were deeply moved by a sense of the sin that crucified the Son of God. They were convicted. They saw the steps to be taken in conversion; they felt the power of the gospel; their hearts were made tender as they saw the sweetness of the love of God. They beheld the beauty of the character of Christ. But with the many it was all in vain. They would not surrender their own habits and character. They would not put off the garments of earth in order to be clothed with the robe of heaven. Their hearts were given to covetousness. They loved the associations of the world more than they loved their God.

Solemn will be the day of final decision. In prophetic vision the apostle John describes it: "I saw a great white throne, and Him that sat on it, from whose face the earth and the heaven fled away; and there was found no place for them. And I saw the dead, small and great, stand before God; and the books were opened; and another book was opened, which is the book of life; and the dead were judged out of those things which were written in the books, according to their works." Revelation 20:11, 12.

Sad will be the retrospect in that day when men stand face to face with eternity. The whole life will present itself just as it has been. The world's pleasures, riches, and honors will not then seem so important. Men will then see that the righteousness they despised is alone of value. They will see that they have fashioned their characters under the deceptive allurements of Satan. The garments they have chosen are the badge of their allegiance to the first great apostate. Then they will see the results of their choice. They will have a knowledge of what it means to transgress the commandments of God.

There will be no future probation in which to prepare for eternity. It is in this life that we are to put on the robe of Christ's righteousness. This is our only opportunity to form characters for the home which Christ has made ready for those who obey His commandments.

The days of our probation are fast closing. The end is near. To us the warning is given, "Take heed to yourselves, lest at any time your hearts be overcharged with surfeiting, and drunkenness, and cares of this life, and so that day come upon you unawares." Luke 21:34. Beware lest it find you unready. Take heed lest you be found at the King's feast without a wedding garment.

"In such an hour as ye think not the Son of man cometh." "Blessed is he that watcheth, and keepeth his garments, lest he walk naked, and they see his shame." Matthew 14:44; Revelation 16:15.

"Come, ye blessed of My Father, inherit the kingdom prepared for you from the foundation of the world" (Matt. 25:34).

Based on Luke 16:1-9

THE WISE EMBEZZLER

Christ's coming was at a time of intense worldliness. Men were subordinating the eternal to the temporal, the claims of the future to the affairs of the present. They were mistaking phantoms for realities, and realities for phantoms. They did not by faith behold the unseen world. Satan presented before them the things of this life as all-attractive and all-absorbing, and they gave heed to his temptations.

Christ came to change this order of things. He sought to break the spell by which men were infatuated and ensnared. In His teaching He sought to adjust the claims of heaven and earth, to turn men's thoughts from the present to the future. From their pursuit of the things of time, He called them to make provision for eternity.

"There was a certain rich man," He said, "which had a steward; and the same was accused unto him that he had wasted his goods." The rich man had left all his possessions in the hands of this servant; but the servant was unfaithful, and the master was convinced that he was being systematically robbed. He determined to retain him no longer in his service, and he called for an investigation of his accounts. "How is it," he said, "that I hear this of thee? Give an account of thy stewardship; for thou mayest be no longer steward."

With the prospect of discharge before him, the steward saw three paths open to his choice. He must labor, beg, or starve. And he said within himself, "What shall I do? for my lord taketh away from me the stewardship: I cannot dig; to beg I am ashamed. I am resolved what to do, that, when I am put out of the stewardship, they may receive me into their houses. So he called every one of his lord's debtors unto him, and said unto the first, How much owest thou unto my lord? And he said, An hundred measures of oil. And he said unto him, Take thy bill, and sit down quickly, and write fifty. Then said he to another, And how much owest thou? And he said, An hundred measures of wheat. And he said unto him, Take thy bill, and write fourscore."

This unfaithful servant made others sharers with him in his dishonesty. He defrauded his master to advantage them, and by accepting this advantage they placed themselves under obligation to receive him as a friend into their homes.

"And the lord commended the unjust steward, because he had done wisely." The worldly man praised the sharpness of the man who had defrauded him. But the rich man's commendation was not the commendation of God.

Christ did not commend the unjust steward, but He made use of a well-known occurrence to illustrate the lesson He desired to teach. "Make to yourselves friends by means of the mammon of unrighteousness," He said; "that when it shall fail, they may receive you into the eternal tabernacles." R.V.

Christ was seeking by every means to win them to higher aims and nobler principles.

The Saviour had been censured by the Pharisees for mingling with publicans and sinners. But His interest in them was not lessened, nor did His efforts for them cease. He saw that their employment brought them into temptation. They were surrounded by enticements to evil. The first wrong step was easy, and the descent was rapid to greater dishonesty and increased crimes. Christ was seeking by every means to win them to higher aims and nobler principles. This purpose He had in mind in the story of the unfaithful steward. There had been among the publicans just such a case as that represented in the parable, and in Christ's description they recognized their own practices. Their attention was arrested, and from the picture of their own dishonest practices many of them learned a lesson of spiritual truth.

The parable was, however, spoken directly to the disciples. To them first the leaven of truth was imparted, and through them it was to reach others. Much of Christ's teaching the disciples did not at first understand, and often His lessons seemed to be almost forgotten. But under the influence of the Holy Spirit these truths were afterward revived with distinctness, and through the disciples they were brought vividly before the new converts who were added to the church.

And the Saviour was speaking also to the Pharisees. He did not relinquish the hope that they would perceive the force of His words. Many had been deeply convicted, and as they should hear the truth under the dictation of the Holy Spirit, not a few would become believers in Christ.

The Pharisees had tried to bring Christ into disrepute by accusing Him of mingling with publicans and sinners. Now He turns the rebuke on these accusers. The scene known to have taken place among the publicans He holds up before the Pharisees both as representing their course of action and as showing the only way in which they can redeem their errors.

To the unfaithful steward his lord's goods had been entrusted for benevolent purposes; but he had used them for himself. So with Israel. God had chosen the seed of Abraham. With a high arm He had delivered them from bondage in Egypt. He had made them the depositaries of sacred truth for the blessing of the world. He had entrusted to them the living oracles that they might communicate the light to others. But His stewards had used these gifts to enrich and exalt themselves.

The Pharisees, filled with self-importance and self-righteousness, were misapplying the goods lent them by God to use for His glory.

The servant in the parable had made no provision for the future. The goods entrusted to him for the benefit of others he had used for himself; but he had thought only of the present. When the stewardship should be taken from him he would have nothing to call his own. But his master's goods were still in his hands, and he determined to use them so as to secure himself against future want. To accomplish this he must work on a new plan. Instead of gathering for himself, he must impart to others. Thus he might secure friends, who, when he should be cast out, would receive him. So with the Pharisees. The stewardship was soon to be taken from them, and they were called upon to provide for the future. Only by seeking the good of others could they benefit themselves. Only by imparting God's gifts in the present life could they provide for eternity.

After relating the parable Christ said, "The children of this world are in their generation wiser than the children of light." That is, worldly-wise men display more wisdom and earnestness in serving themselves than do the professed children of God in their service to Him. So it was in Christ's day. So it is now. Look at the life of many who claim to be Christians. The Lord has endowed them with capabilities, and power, and influence; He has entrusted them with money, that they may be co-workers with Him in the great redemption. All His gifts are to be used in blessing humanity, in relieving the suffering and the needy. We are to feed the hungry, to clothe the naked, to care for the widow and the fatherless, to minister to the distressed and downtrodden. God never meant that the widespread misery in the world should exist. He never meant that one man should have an abundance of the luxuries of life, while the children of others should cry for bread. The means over and above the actual necessities of life are entrusted to man to do good, to bless humanity. The Lord says, "Sell that ye have, and give alms." Luke 12:33. Be "ready to distribute, willing to communicate." 1 Timothy 6:18. "When thou makest a feast, call the poor, the maimed, the lame, the blind." Luke 14:13. "Loose the bands of wickedness," "undo the heavy burdens," "let the oppressed go free," "break every yoke." "Deal thy bread to the hungry," "bring the poor that are cast out to thy house." "When thou seest the naked, . . . cover him." "Satisfy the afflicted soul." Isaiah 58:6, 7, 10. "Go ye into all the world, and preach the gospel to every creature." Mark 16:15. These are the Lord's commands. Are the great body of professed Christians doing this work?

All His gifts are to be used in blessing humanity, in relieving the suffering and the needy.

Alas, how many are appropriating to themselves the gifts of God! How many are adding house to house and land to land. How many are spending their money for pleasure, for the gratification of appetite, for extravagant houses, furniture, and dress. Their fellow beings are left to misery and crime, to disease and death. Multitudes are perishing without one pitying look, one word or deed of sympathy.

Men are guilty of robbery toward God. Their selfish use of means robs the Lord of the glory that should be reflected back to Him in the relief of suffering humanity and the salvation of souls. They are embezzling His entrusted goods. The Lord declares, "I will come near to you to judgment; and I will be a swift witness against . . . those that oppress the hireling in his wages, the widow, and the fatherless, and that turn aside the stranger from his right." "Will a man rob God? Yet ye have robbed Me. But ye say, Wherein have we robbed Thee? In tithes and offerings. Ye are cursed with a curse: for ye have robbed Me, even this whole nation." Malachi 3:5, 8, 9. "Go to now, ye rich men, . . . your riches are corrupted, and your garments are moth-eaten. Your gold and silver is cankered, and the rust of them shall be a witness against you. . . . Ye have heaped treasure together for the last days." "Ye have lived in pleasure on the earth, and been wanton." "Behold, the hire of the laborers who have reaped down your fields, which is of you kept back by fraud, crieth: and the cries of them which have reaped are entered into the ears of the Lord of sabaoth." James 5:1-3, 5, 4.

Riches rightly employed will accomplish great good. Souls will be won to Christ.

Everyone will be required to render up his entrusted gifts. In the day of final judgment men's hoarded wealth will be worthless to them. They have nothing they can call their own.

Those who spend their lives in laying up worldly treasure show less wisdom, less thought and care for their eternal well-being, than did the unjust steward for his earthly support. Less wise than the children of this world in their generation are these professed children of the light. These are they of whom the prophet declared, in his vision of the great judgment day, "A man shall cast the idols of his silver, and the idols of his gold [margin], which they made each one for himself to worship, to the moles and to the bats; to go into the clefts of the rocks, and into the tops of the ragged rocks, for fear of the Lord, and for the glory of His majesty, when He ariseth to shake terribly the earth." Isaiah 2:20, 21.

"Make to yourselves friends by means of the mammon of unrighteousness," Christ says, "that when it shall fail, they may receive you into the eternal tabernacles." R. V. God and Christ and angels are all ministering to the afflicted, the suffering, and the sinful. Give yourself to God for this work, use His gifts for this purpose, and you enter into partnership with heavenly beings. Your heart will throb in sympathy with theirs. You will be assimilated to them in character. To you these dwellers in the eternal tabernacles will not be strangers. When earthly things shall have passed away, the watchers at heaven's gates will bid you welcome.

And the means used to bless others will bring returns. Riches rightly employed will accomplish great good. Souls will be won to Christ. He who follows Christ's plan of life will see in the courts of God those for whom he has labored and sacrificed on earth. Gratefully will the ransomed ones remember those who have been instrumental in their salvation. Precious will heaven be to those who have been faithful in the work of saving souls.

The lesson of this parable is for all. Everyone will be held responsible for the grace given him through Christ. Life is too solemn to be absorbed in temporal or earthly matters. The Lord desires that we shall communicate to others that which the eternal and unseen communicates to us.

Every year millions upon millions of human souls are passing into eternity unwarned and unsaved. From hour to hour in our varied life opportunities to reach and save souls are opened to us. These opportunities are continually coming and going. God desires us to make the most of them. Days, weeks, and months are passing; we have one day, one week, one month less in which to do our work. A few more years at the longest, and the voice which we cannot refuse to answer will be heard saying, "Give an account of thy stewardship."

Christ calls upon every one to consider. Make an honest reckoning. Put into one scale Jesus, which means eternal treasure, life, truth, heaven, and the joy of Christ in souls redeemed; put into the other every attraction the world can offer. Into one scale put the loss of your own soul, and the souls of those whom you might have been instrumental in saving; into the other, for yourself and for them, a life that measures with the life of God. Weigh for time and for eternity. While you are thus engaged, Christ speaks: "What shall it profit a man, if he shall gain the whole world, and lose his own soul?" Mark 8:36.

God desires us to choose the heavenly in place of the earthly. He opens before us the possibilities of a heavenly investment. He would give encouragement to our loftiest aims, security to our choicest treasure. He declares, "I will make a man more precious than fine gold; even a man than the golden wedge of Ophir." Isaiah 13:12. When the riches that moth devours and rust corrupts shall be swept away, Christ's followers can rejoice in their heavenly treasure, the riches that are imperishable.

Better than all the friendship of the world is the friendship of Christ's redeemed. Better than a title to the noblest palace on earth is a title to the mansion our Lord has gone to prepare. And better than all the words of earthly praise will be the Saviour's words to His faithful servants, "Come, ye blessed of My Father, inherit the kingdom prepared for you from the foundation of the world." Matthew 25:34.

To those who have squandered His goods Christ still gives opportunity to secure lasting riches. He says, "Give, and it shall be given unto you." "Provide yourselves bags which wax not old, a treasure in the heavens that faileth not, where no thief approacheth, neither moth corrupteth." Luke 6:38; 12:33. "Charge them that are rich in this world, . . . that they do good, that they be rich in good works, ready to distribute, willing to communicate; laying up in store for themselves a good foundation against the time to come, that they may lay hold on eternal life." 1 Timothy 6:17-19.

Then let your property go beforehand to heaven. Lay up your treasures beside the throne of God. Make sure your title to the unsearchable riches of Christ. "Make to yourselves friends by means of the mammon of unrighteousness; that, when it shall fail, they may receive you into the eternal tabernacles." R. V

"These things I command you, that ye love one another" (John 15:17).

ARE YOU MY NEIGHBOR?

Among the Jews the question, "Who is my neighbor?" caused endless dispute. They had no doubt as to the heathen and the Samaritans. These were strangers and enemies. But where should the distinction be made among the people of their own nation and among the different classes of society? Whom should the priest, the rabbi, the elder, regard as neighbor? They spent their lives in a round of ceremonies to make themselves pure. Contact with the ignorant and careless multitude, they taught, would cause defilement that would require wearisome effort to remove. Were they to regard the "unclean" as neighbors?

This question Christ answered in the parable of the good Samaritan. He showed that our neighbor does not mean merely one of the church or faith of which we belong. It has no reference to race, color, or class distinction. Our neighbor is every person who needs our help. Our neighbor is every soul who is wounded and bruised by the adversary. Our neighbor is every one who is the property of God.

The parable of the good Samaritan was called forth by a question put to Christ by a doctor of the law. As the Saviour was teaching, "a certain lawyer stood up, and tempted Him saying, Master, what shall I do to inherit eternal life?" The Pharisees had suggested this question to the lawyer in the hope that they might entrap Christ in His words, and they listened eagerly for His answer. But the Saviour entered into no controversy. He required the answer from the questioner himself. "What is written in the law?" He asked, "How readest thou?" The Jews still accused Jesus of lightly regarding the law given from Sinai, but He turned the question of salvation upon the keeping of God's commandments.

The lawyer said, "Thou shalt love the Lord thy God with all thy heart, and with all thy soul, and with all thy strength, and with all thy mind; and thy neighbor as thyself." "Thou hast answered right," Christ said: "this do, and thou shalt live."

The lawyer was not satisfied with the position and works of the Pharisees. He had been studying the Scriptures with a desire to learn their real meaning. He had a vital interest in the matter, and he asked in sincerity, "What shall I do?" In his answer as to the requirements of the law, he passed by all the mass of ceremonial and ritualistic precepts. For these he claimed no value, but presented the two great principles on which hang all the law and the prophets. The Saviour's commendation of this answer placed Him on vantage ground with the rabbis. They could not condemn Him for sanctioning that which had been advanced by an expositor of the law.

"This do, and thou shalt live," Christ said. In His teaching He ever presented the law as a divine unity, showing that it is impossible to keep one precept and break another, for the same principle runs through all. Man's destiny will be determined by his obedience to the whole law.

Christ knew that no one could obey the law in his own strength.

Christ knew that no one could obey the law in his own strength. He desired to lead the lawyer to clearer and more critical research that he might find the truth. Only by accepting the virtue and grace of Christ can we keep the law. Belief in the propitiation for sin enables fallen man to love God with his whole heart and his neighbor as himself.

The lawyer knew that he had kept neither the first four nor the last six commandments. He was convicted under Christ's searching words, but instead of confessing his sin he tried to excuse it. Rather than acknowledge the truth, he endeavored to show how difficult of fulfillment the commandment is. Thus he hoped both to parry conviction and to vindicate himself in the eyes of the people. The Saviour's words had shown that his question was needless, since he was able to answer it himself. Yet he put another question, saying, "Who is my neighbor?"

Again Christ refused to be drawn into controversy, He answered the question by relating an incident, the memory of which was fresh in the minds of His hearers. "A certain man," He said, "went down from Jerusalem to Jericho, and fell among thieves, which stripped him of his raiment, and wounded him, and departed, leaving him half dead."

In journeying from Jerusalem to Jericho the traveler had to pass through a portion of the wilderness of Judea. The road led down a wild, rocky ravine, which was infested with robbers, and was often the scene of violence. It was here that the traveler was attacked, stripped of all that was valuable, and left half dead by the wayside. As he lay thus, a priest came that way; he saw the man lying wounded and bruised, weltering in his own blood; but he left him without rendering any assistance. He "passed by on the other side." Then a Levite appeared. Curious to know what had happened, he stopped and looked at the sufferer. He was convinced of what he ought to do, but it was not an agreeable duty. He wished that he had not come that way so that he would not have seen the wounded man. He persuaded himself that the case was no concern of his, and he too "passed by on the other side."

But a Samaritan, traveling the same road, saw the sufferer, and he did the work that the others had refused to do. With gentleness and kindness he ministered to the wounded man. "When he saw him, he had compassion on him, and went to him, and bound up his wounds, pouring in oil and wine, and set him on his own beast, and brought him to an inn, and took care of him. And on the morrow when he departed, he took out two pence, and gave them to the host, and said unto him, Take care of him; and whatsoever thou spendest more, when I come again, I will repay thee." The priest and the Levite both professed piety, but the Samaritan showed that he was truly converted. It was no more agreeable for him to do the work than for the priest and Levite, but in spirit and works he proved himself to be in harmony with God.

In giving this lesson Christ presented the principles of the law in a direct, forcible way, showing His hearers that they had neglected to carry out these principles. His words were so definite and pointed that the listeners could find no opportunity to cavil. The lawyer found in the lesson nothing that he could criticize. His prejudice in regard to Christ was removed. But he had not overcome his national dislike sufficiently to give credit to the Samaritan by name. When Christ asked, "Which now of these three, thinkest thou, was neighbour unto him that fell among the thieves?" he answered, "He that shewed mercy on him."

"Then said Jesus unto him, Go, and do thou likewise." Show the same tender kindness to those in need. Thus you will give evidence that you keep the whole law.

The great difference between the Jews and the Samaritans was a difference in religious belief, a question as to what constitutes true worship. The Pharisees would say nothing good of the Samaritans, but poured their bitterest curses upon them. So strong was the antipathy between the Jews and the Samaritans that to the Samaritan woman it seemed a strange thing for Christ to ask her for a drink. "How is it," she said, "that Thou, being a Jew, askest drink of me, which am a woman of Samaria? For," adds the evangelist, "the Jews have no dealings with the Samaritans." John 4:9. And when the Jews were so filled with murderous hatred against Christ that they rose up in the temple to stone Him, they could find no better words by which to express their hatred than, "Say we not well that Thou art a Samaritan, and hast a devil?" John 8:48. Yet the priest and the Levite neglected the very work the Lord had enjoined on them, leaving a hated and despised Samaritan to minister to one of their own countrymen.

The Samaritan had fulfilled the command, "Thou shalt love thy neighbour as thyself," thus showing that he was more righteous than those by whom he was denounced. Risking his own life, he had treated the wounded man as his brother. This Samaritan represents Christ. Our Saviour manifested for us a love that the love of man can never equal. When we were bruised and dying He had pity upon us. He did not pass us by on the other side, and leave us, helpless and hopeless, to perish. He did not remain in His holy, happy home, where He was beloved by all the heavenly host. He beheld our sore need, He undertook our case, and identified His interests with those of humanity. He died to save His enemies. He prayed for His murderers. Pointing to His own example, He says to His followers, "These things I command you, that ye love one another," "as I have loved you, that ye also love one another." John 15:17; 13:34.

When we were bruised and dying He had pity upon us.

The priest and the Levite had been for worship to the temple whose service was appointed by God Himself. To participate in that service was a great and exalted privilege, and the priest and Levite felt that having been thus honored, it was beneath them to minister to an unknown sufferer by the wayside. Thus they neglected the special opportunity which God had offered them as His agents to bless a fellow being.

Many today are making a similar mistake. They separate their duties into two distinct classes. The one class is made up of great things, to be regulated by the law of God; the other class is made up of so-called little things, in which the command, "Thou shalt love thy neighbour as thyself," is ignored. This sphere of work is left to caprice, subject to inclination or impulse. Thus the character is marred, and the religion of Christ misrepresented.

The mere profession of religion abounds, but it has little weight.

There are those who would think it lowering to their dignity to minister to suffering humanity. Many look with indifference and contempt upon those who have laid the temple of the soul in ruins. Others neglect the poor from a different motive. They are working, as they believe, in the cause of Christ, seeking to build up some worthy enterprise. They feel that they are doing a great work, and they cannot stop to notice the wants of the needy and distressed. In advancing their supposedly great work they may even oppress the poor. They may place them in hard and trying circumstances, deprive them of their rights, or neglect their needs. Yet they feel that all this is justifiable because they are, as they think, advancing the cause of Christ.

Many will allow a brother or a neighbor to struggle unaided under adverse circumstances. Because they profess to be Christians he may be led to think that in their cold selfishness they are representing Christ. Because the Lord's professed servants are not in cooperation with Him, the love of God, which should flow forth from them, is in great degree cut off from their fellow men. And a large revenue of praise and thanksgiving from human hearts and human lips is prevented from flowing back to God. He is robbed of the glory due to His holy name. He is robbed of the souls for whom Christ died, souls whom He longs to bring into His kingdom to dwell in His presence through endless ages.

Divine truth exerts little influence upon the world, when it should exert much influence through our practice. The mere profession of religion abounds, but it has little weight. We may claim to be followers of Christ, we may claim to believe every truth in the word of God; but this will do our neighbor no good unless our belief is carried into our daily life. Our profession may be as high as heaven, but it will save neither ourselves nor our fellow men unless we are Christians. A right example will do more to benefit the world than all our profession.

By no selfish practices can the cause of Christ be served. His cause is the cause of the oppressed and the poor. In the hearts of His professed followers there is need of the tender sympathy of Christ—a deeper love for those whom He has so valued as to give His own life for their salvation. These souls are precious, infinitely more precious than any other offering we can bring to God. To bend every energy toward some apparently great work, while we neglect the needy or turn the stranger from his right, is not a service that will meet His approval.

The sanctification of the soul by the working of the Holy Spirit is the implanting of Christ's nature in humanity. Gospel religion is Christ in the life—a living, active principle. It is the grace of Christ revealed in character and wrought out in good works. The principles of the gospel cannot be disconnected from any department of practical life. Every line of Christian experience and labor is to be a representation of the life of Christ.

Love is the basis of godliness. Whatever the profession, no man has pure love to God unless he has unselfish love for his brother. But we can never come into possession of this spirit by *trying* to love others. What is needed is the love of Christ in the heart. When self is merged in Christ, love springs forth spontaneously. The completeness of Christian character is attained when the impulse to help and bless others springs constantly from within—when the sunshine of heaven fills the heart and is revealed in the countenance.

It is not possible for the heart in which Christ abides to be destitute of love. If we love God because He first loved us, we shall love all for whom Christ died. We cannot come in touch with divinity without coming in touch with humanity, for in Him who sits upon the throne of the universe divinity and humanity are combined. Connected with Christ, we are connected with our fellow men by the golden links of the chain of love. Then the pity and compassion of Christ will be manifest in our life. We shall not wait to have the needy and unfortunate brought to us. We shall not need to be entreated to feel for the woes of others. It will be as natural for us to minister to the needy and suffering as it was for Christ to go about doing good.

Wherever there is an impulse of love and sympathy, wherever the heart reaches out to bless and uplift others, there is revealed the working of God's Holy Spirit. In the depths of heathenism men who have had no knowledge of the written law of God, who have never even heard the name of Christ, have been kind to His servants, protecting them at the risk of their own lives. Their acts show the working of a divine power. The Holy Spirit has implanted the grace of Christ in the heart of the savage, quickening his sympathies contrary to his nature, contrary to his education. The "Light, which lighteth every man that cometh into the world" (John 1:9), is shining in his soul; and this light, if heeded, will guide his feet to the kingdom of God.

Whatever the profession, no man has pure love to God unless he has unselfish love for his brother.

The glory of heaven is in lifting up the fallen, comforting the distressed. And wherever Christ abides in human hearts He will be revealed in the same way. Wherever it acts the religion of Christ will bless. Wherever it works there is brightness.

No distinction on account of nationality, race, or caste is recognized by God. He is the Maker of all mankind. All men are of one family by creation, and all are one through redemption. Christ came to demolish every wall of partition, to throw open every compartment of the temple, that every soul may have free access to God. His love is so broad, so deep, so full, that it penetrates everywhere. It lifts out of Satan's circle the poor souls who have been deluded by his deceptions. It places them within reach of the throne of God, the throne encircled by the rainbow of promise.

In Christ there is neither Jew nor Greek, bond nor free. All are brought nigh by His precious blood. (Galatians 3:28; Ephesians 2:13.)

We should enter into the joys and cares of both high and low, rich and poor.

Whatever the difference in religious belief, a call from suffering humanity must be heard and answered. Where bitterness of feeling exists because of difference in religion, much good may be done by personal service. Loving ministry will break down prejudice, and win souls to God.

We should anticipate the sorrows, the difficulties, the troubles of others. We should enter into the joys and cares of both high and low, rich and poor. "Freely ye have received," Christ says, "freely give." Matthew 10:8. All around us are poor, tried souls that need sympathizing words and helpful deeds. There are widows who need sympathy and assistance. There are orphans whom Christ has bidden His followers receive as a trust from God. Too often these are passed by with neglect. They may be ragged, uncouth, and seemingly in every way unattractive; yet they are God's property. They have been bought with a price, and they are as precious in His sight as we are. They are members of God's great household, and Christians as His stewards are responsible for them. "Their souls," He says, "will I require at thine hand."

Sin is the greatest of all evils, and it is ours to pity and help the sinner. But not all can be reached in the same way. There are many who hide their soul hunger. These would be greatly helped by a tender word or a kind remembrance. There are others who are in the greatest need, yet they know it not. They do not realize the terrible destitution of the soul. Multitudes are so sunken in sin that they have lost the sense of eternal realities, lost the similitude of God, and they hardly know whether they have souls to be saved or not. They have neither faith in God nor confidence in man. Many of these can be reached only through acts of disinterested kindness. Their physical wants must first be cared for. They must be fed, cleansed, and decently clothed. As they see the evidence of your unselfish love, it will be easier for them to believe in the love of Christ.

There are many who err, and who feel their shame and their folly. They look upon their mistakes and errors until they are driven almost to desperation. These souls we are not to neglect. When one has to swim against the stream, there is all the force of the current driving him back. Let a helping hand then be held out to him as was the Elder Brother's hand to the sinking Peter. Speak to him hopeful words, words that will establish confidence and awaken love.

Thy brother, sick in spirit, needs thee, as thou thyself hast needed a brother's love. He needs the experience of one who has been as weak as he, one who can sympathize with him and help him. The knowledge of our own weakness should help us to help another in his bitter need. Never should we pass by one suffering soul without seeking to impart to him the comfort wherewith we are comforted of God.

It is fellowship with Christ, personal contact with a living Saviour, that enables the mind and heart and soul to triumph over the lower nature. Tell the wanderer of an almighty hand that will hold him up, of an infinite humanity in Christ that pities him. It is not enough for him to believe in law and force, things that have no pity, and never hear the cry for help. He needs to clasp a hand that is warm, to trust in a heart full of tenderness. Keep his mind stayed upon the thought of a divine presence ever beside him, ever looking upon him with pitying love. Bid him think of a Father's heart that ever grieves over sin, of a Father's hand stretched out still, of a Father's voice saying, "Let him take hold of My strength, that he may make peace with Me; and he shall make peace." Isaiah 27:5.

As you engage in this work, you have companions unseen by human eyes. Angels of heaven were beside the Samaritan who cared for the wounded stranger. Angels from the heavenly courts stand by all who do God's service in ministering to their fellow men. And you have the cooperation of Christ Himself. He is the Restorer, and as you work under His supervision, you will see great results.

Upon your faithfulness in this work not only the well-being of others but your own eternal destiny depends. Christ is seeking to uplift all who will be lifted to companionship with Himself, that we may be one with Him as He is one with the Father. He permits us to come in contact with suffering and calamity in order to call us out of our selfishness; He seeks to develop in us the attributes of His character—compassion, tenderness, and love. By accepting this work of ministry we place ourselves in His school, to be fitted for the courts of God. By rejecting it, we reject His instruction, and choose eternal separation from His presence.

"If thou wilt keep My charge," the Lord declares, "I will give thee places to walk among these that stand by"—even among the angels that surround His throne. (Zechariah 3:7.) By cooperating with heavenly beings in their work on earth, we are preparing for their companionship in heaven. "Ministering spirits, sent forth to minister for them who shall be heirs of salvation" (Hebrews 1:14), angels in heaven will welcome those who on earth have lived "not to be ministered unto, but to minister." Matthew 20:28. In this blessed companionship we shall learn, to our eternal joy, all that is wrapped up in the question, "Who is my neighbour?"

"Not by might, nor by power, but by My spirit, saith the Lord of hosts" (Zech. 4:6).

To Meet the Bridegroom

Christ with His disciples is seated upon the Mount of Olives. The sun has set behind the mountains, and the heavens are curtained with the shades of evening. In full view is a dwelling house lighted up brilliantly as if for some festive scene. The light streams from the openings, and an expectant company wait around, indicating that a marriage procession is soon to appear. In many parts of the East, wedding festivities are held in the evening. The bridegroom goes forth to meet his bride and bring her to his home. By torchlight the bridal party proceed from her father's house to his own, where a feast is provided for the invited guests. In the scene upon which Christ looks, a company are awaiting the appearance of the bridal party, intending to join the procession.

Lingering near the bride's house are ten young women robed in white. Each carries a lighted lamp and a small flagon for oil. All are anxiously watching for the appearance of the bridegroom. But there is a delay. Hour after hour passes; the watchers become weary and fall asleep. At midnight the cry is heard, "Behold, the bridegroom cometh; go ye out to meet him." The sleepers, suddenly awaking, spring to their feet. They see the procession moving on, bright with torches and glad with music. They hear the voice of the bridegroom and the voice of the bride. The ten maidens seize their lamps and begin to trim them, in haste to go forth. But five have neglected to fill their flasks with oil. They did not anticipate so long a delay, and they have not prepared for the emergency. In distress they appeal to their wiser companions, saying, "Give us of your oil; for our lamps are going out" (margin). But the waiting five, with their freshly trimmed lamps, have emptied their flagons. They have no oil to spare, and they answer, "Not so; lest there be not enough for us and you: but go ye rather to them that sell, and buy for yourselves."

While they went to buy, the procession moved on, and left them behind. The five with lighted lamps joined the throng and entered the house with the bridal train, and the door was shut. When the foolish virgins reached the banqueting hall, they received an unexpected denial. The master of the feast declared, "I know you not." They were left standing without, in the empty street, in the blackness of the night.

As Christ sat looking upon the party that waited for the bridegroom, He told His disciples the story of the ten virgins, by their experience illustrating the experience of the church that shall live just before His second coming.

The two classes of watchers represent the two classes who profess to be waiting for their Lord. They are called virgins because they profess a pure faith. By the lamps is represented the word of God. The psalmist says, "Thy word is a lamp

Without the Spirit of God a knowledge of His word is of no avail.

unto my feet, and a light unto my path." Psalm 119:105. The oil is a symbol of the Holy Spirit. Thus the Spirit is represented in the prophecy of Zechariah. "The angel that talked with me came again," he says, "and waked me, as a man that is wakened out of his sleep, and said unto me, What seest thou? And I said, I have looked, and behold a candlestick all of gold, with a bowl upon the top of it, and his seven lamps thereon, and seven pipes to the seven lamps, which are upon the top thereof; and two olive trees by it, one upon the right side of the bowl, and the other upon the left side thereof. So I answered and spake to the angel that talked with me, saying, What are these, my lord? . . . Then he answered and spake unto me, saying, This is the word of the Lord unto Zerubbabel, saying, Not by might, nor by power, but by My spirit, saith the Lord of hosts. . . . And I answered again, and said unto him, What be these two olive branches which through the two golden pipes empty the golden oil out of themselves? . . . Then said he, These are the two anointed ones, that stand by the Lord of the whole earth." Zechariah 4:1-14.

From the two olive trees the golden oil was emptied through the golden pipes into the bowl of the candlestick, and thence into the golden lamps that gave light to the sanctuary. So from the holy ones that stand in God's presence His Spirit is imparted to the human instrumentalities who are consecrated to His service. The mission of the two anointed ones is to communicate to God's people that heavenly grace which alone can make His word a lamp to the feet and a light to the path. "Not by might, nor by power, but by My spirit, saith the Lord of hosts." Zechariah 4:6.

In the parable, all the ten virgins went out to meet the bridegroom. All had lamps and vessels for oil. For a time there was seen no difference between them. So with the church that lives just before Christ's second coming. All have a knowledge of the Scriptures. All have heard the message of Christ's near approach, and confidently expect His appearing. But as in the parable, so it is now. A time of waiting intervenes, faith is tried; and when the cry is heard, "Behold, the Bridegroom cometh; go ye out to meet Him," many are unready. They have no oil in their vessels with their lamps. They are destitute of the Holy Spirit.

Without the Spirit of God a knowledge of His word is of no avail. The theory of truth, unaccompanied by the Holy Spirit, cannot quicken the soul or sanctify the heart. One may be familiar with the commands and promises of the Bible; but unless the Spirit of God sets the truth home, the character will not be transformed. Without the enlightenment of the Spirit, men will not be able to distinguish truth from error, and they will fall under the masterful temptations of Satan.

The class represented by the foolish virgins are not hypocrites. They have a regard for the truth, they have advocated the truth, they are attracted to those who believe the truth; but they have not yielded themselves to the Holy Spirit's working. They have not fallen upon the Rock, Christ Jesus, and permitted their old nature to be broken up. This class are represented also by the stony-ground hearers. They receive the word with readiness, but they fail of assimilating its principles. Its influence is not abiding. The Spirit works upon man's heart, according to his desire and consent implanting in him a new nature; but the class represented by the foolish virgins have been content with a superficial work. They do not know God. They have not studied His character; they have not held communion with Him; therefore they do not know how to trust, how to look and live. Their service to God degenerates into a form. "They come unto thee as the people cometh, and they sit before thee as My people, and they hear thy words, but they will not do them; for with their mouth they show much love, but their heart goeth after their covetousness." Ezekiel 33:31. The apostle Paul points out that this will be the special characteristic of those who live just before Christ's second coming. He says, "In the last days perilous times shall come: for men shall be lovers of their own selves; . . . lovers of pleasures more than lovers of God; having a form of godliness, but denying the power thereof." 2 Timothy 3:1-5.

This is the class that in time of peril are found crying, Peace and safety. They lull their hearts into security, and dream not of danger. When startled from their lethargy, they discern their destitution, and entreat others to supply their lack; but in spiritual things no man can make up another's deficiency. The grace of God has been freely offered to every soul. The message of the gospel has been heralded, "Let him that is athirst come. And whosoever will, let him take the water of life freely." Revelation 22:17. But character is not transferable. No man can believe for another. No man can receive the Spirit for another. No man can impart to another the character which is the fruit of the Spirit's working. "Though Noah, Daniel, and Job were in it [the land], as I live, saith the Lord God, they shall deliver neither son nor daughter; they shall but deliver their own souls by their righteousness." Ezekiel 14:20.

Character is not transferable. No man can believe for another.

It is in a crisis that character is revealed. When the earnest voice proclaimed at midnight, "Behold, the bridegroom cometh; go ye out to meet him," and the sleeping virgins were roused from their slumbers, it was seen who had made preparation for the event. Both parties were taken unawares; but one was prepared for the emergency, and the other was found without preparation. So now, a sudden and unlooked-for calamity, something that brings the soul face to face with death, will show whether there is any real faith in the promises of God. It will show whether the soul is sustained by grace.

The great final test comes at the close of human probation, when it will be too late for the soul's need to be supplied.

The ten virgins are watching in the evening of this earth's history. All claim to be Christians. All have a call, a name, a lamp, and all profess to be doing God's service. All apparently wait for Christ's appearing. But five are unready. Five will be found surprised, dismayed, outside the banquet hall.

At the final day, many will claim admission to Christ's kingdom, saying, "We have eaten and drunk in Thy presence, and Thou hast taught in our streets." "Lord, Lord, have we not

Saddest of all words that ever fell on mortal ear are those words of doom, "I know you not."

prophesied in Thy name? and in Thy name have cast out devils? and in Thy name done many wonderful works?" But the answer is, "I tell you, I know you not whence ye are; depart from Me." Luke 13:26, 27; Matthew 7:22. In this life they have not entered into fellowship with Christ; therefore they know not the language of heaven, they are strangers to its joy. "What man knoweth the things of a man, save the spirit of man which is in him? even so the things of God knoweth no man, but the Spirit of God." 1 Corinthians 2:11.

Saddest of all words that ever fell on mortal ear are those words of doom, "I know you not." The fellowship of the Spirit, which you have slighted, could alone make you one with the joyous throng at the marriage feast. In that scene you cannot participate. Its light would fall on blinded eyes, its melody upon deaf ears. Its love and joy could awake no chord of gladness in the world-benumbed heart. You are shut out from heaven by your own unfitness for its companionship.

We cannot be ready to meet the Lord by waking when the cry is heard, "Behold, the Bridegroom!" and then gathering up our empty lamps to have them replenished. We cannot keep Christ apart from our lives here, and yet be fitted for His companionship in heaven.

In the parable the wise virgins had oil in their vessels with their lamps. Their light burned with undimmed flame through the night of watching. It helped to swell the illumination for the bridegroom's honor. Shining out in the darkness, it helped to illuminate the way to the home of the bridegroom, to the marriage feast.

So the followers of Christ are to shed light into the darkness of the world. Through the Holy Spirit, God's word is a light as it becomes a transforming power in the life of the receiver. By implanting in their hearts the principles of His word, the Holy Spirit develops in men the attributes of God. The light of His glory—His character—is to shine forth in His followers. Thus they are to glorify God, to lighten the path to the Bridegroom's home, to the city of God, to the marriage supper of the Lamb.

The coming of the bridegroom was at midnight—the darkest hour. So the coming of Christ will take place in the darkest period of this earth's history. The days of Noah and Lot pictured the condition of the world just before the coming of the Son of man. The Scriptures pointing forward to this time declare that Satan will work with all power and "with all deceivableness of unrighteousness." 2 Thessalonians 2:9, 10. His working is plainly revealed by the rapidly increasing darkness, the multitudinous errors, heresies, and delusions of these last days. Not only is Satan leading the world captive, but his deceptions are leavening the professed churches of our Lord Jesus Christ. The great apostasy will develop into darkness deep as midnight, impenetrable as sackcloth of hair. To God's people it will be a night of trial, a night of weeping, a night of persecution for the truth's sake. But out of that night of darkness God's light will shine.

He causes "the light to shine out of darkness." 2 Corinthians 4:6. When "the earth was without form, and void, and darkness was upon the face of the deep," "the Spirit of God moved upon the face of the waters. And God said, Let there be light; and there was light." Genesis 1:2, 3. So in the night of spiritual darkness, God's word goes forth, "Let there be light." To His people He says, "Arise, shine; for thy light is come, and the glory of the Lord is risen upon thee." Isaiah 60:1.

"Behold," says the Scripture, "the darkness shall cover the earth, and gross darkness the people; but the Lord shall arise upon thee, and His glory shall be seen upon thee." Isaiah 60:2.

It is the darkness of misapprehension of God that is enshrouding the world. Men are losing their knowledge of His character. It has been misunderstood and misinterpreted. At this time a message from God is to be proclaimed, a message illuminating in its influence and saving in its power. His character is to be made known. Into the darkness of the world is to be shed the light of His glory, the light of His goodness, mercy, and truth.

This is the work outlined by the prophet Isaiah in the words, "O Jerusalem, that bringest good tidings, lift up thy voice with strength; lift it up, be not afraid; say unto the cities of Judah, Behold your God! Behold, the Lord God will come with strong hand, and His arm shall rule for Him; behold, His reward is with Him, and His work before Him." Isaiah 40:9, 10.

Those who wait for the Bridegroom's coming are to say to the people, "Behold your God." The last rays of merciful light, the last message of mercy to be given to the world, is a revelation of His character of love. The children of God are to manifest His glory. In their own life and character they are to reveal what the grace of God has done for them.

The children of God are to manifest His glory. In their own life and character they are to reveal what the grace of God has done for them.

The light of the Sun of Righteousness is to shine forth in good works—in words of truth and deeds of holiness.

Christ, the outshining of the Father's glory, came to the world as its light. He came to represent God to men, and of Him it is written that He was anointed "with the Holy Ghost and with power," and "went about doing good." Acts 10:38. In the synagogue at Nazareth He said, "The Spirit of the Lord is upon Me, because He hath anointed Me to preach the gospel to the poor; He hath sent Me to heal the brokenhearted, to preach deliverance to the captives, and recovering of sight to the blind, to set at liberty them that are bruised, to preach the acceptable year of the Lord." Luke 4:18, 19. This was the work He commissioned His disciples to do. "Ye are the light of the world," He said. "Let your light so shine before men, that they may see your good works, and glorify your Father which is in heaven." Matthew 5:14, 16.

This is the work which the prophet Isaiah describes when he says, "Is it not to deal thy bread to the hungry, and that thou bring the poor that are cast out to thy house? When thou seest the naked, that thou cover him; and that thou hide not thyself from thine own flesh? Then shall thy light break forth as the morning, and thine health shall spring forth speedily; and thy righteousness shall go before thee; the glory of the Lord shall be thy reward." Isaiah 58:7, 8.

The message of hope and mercy is to be carried to the ends of the earth.

Thus in the night of spiritual darkness God's glory is to shine forth through His church in lifting up the bowed down and comforting those that mourn.

All around us are heard the wails of a world's sorrow. On every hand are the needy and distressed. It is ours to aid in relieving and softening life's hardships and misery.

Practical work will have far more effect than mere sermonizing. We are to give food to the hungry, clothing to the naked, and shelter to the homeless. And we are called to do more than this. The wants of the soul, only the love of Christ can satisfy. If Christ is abiding in us, our hearts will be full of divine sympathy. The sealed fountains of earnest, Christlike love will be unsealed.

God calls not only for our gifts for the needy, but for our cheerful countenance, our hopeful words, our kindly handclasp. When Christ healed the sick, He laid His hands upon them. So should we come in close touch with those whom we seek to benefit.

There are many from whom hope has departed. Bring back the sunshine to them. Many have lost their courage. Speak to them words of cheer. Pray for them. There are those who need the bread of life. Read to them from the word of God. Upon many is a soul sickness which no earthly balm can reach nor physician heal. Pray for these souls, bring them to Jesus. Tell them that there is a balm in Gilead and a Physician there.

Light is a blessing, a universal blessing, pouring forth its treasures on a world unthankful, unholy, demoralized. So it is with the light of the Sun of Righteousness. The whole earth, wrapped as it is in the darkness of sin, and sorrow, and pain, is to be lighted with the knowledge of God's love. From no sect, rank, or class of people is the light shining from heaven's throne to be excluded.

The message of hope and mercy is to be carried to the ends of the earth. Whosoever will, may reach forth and take hold of God's strength and make peace with Him, and he shall make peace. No longer are the heathen to be wrapped in midnight darkness. The gloom is to disappear before the bright beams of the Sun of Righteousness. The power of hell has been overcome.

But no man can impart that which he himself has not received. In the work of God, humanity can originate nothing. No man can by his own effort make himself a light bearer for God. It was the golden oil emptied by the heavenly messengers into the golden tubes, to be conducted from the golden bowl into the lamps of the sanctuary, that produced a continuous bright and shining light. It is the love of God continually transferred to man that enables him to impart light. Into the hearts of all who are united to God by faith the golden oil of love flows freely, to shine out again in good works, in real, heartfelt service for God.

In the great and measureless gift of the Holy Spirit are contained all of heaven's resources. It is not because of any restriction on the part of God that the riches of His grace do not flow earthward to men. If all were willing to receive, all would become filled with His Spirit.

It is the privilege of every soul to be a living channel through which God can communicate to the world the treasures of His grace, the unsearchable riches of Christ. There is nothing that Christ desires so much as agents who will represent to the world His Spirit and character. There is nothing that the world needs so much as the manifestation through humanity of the Saviour's love. All heaven is waiting for channels through which can be poured the holy oil to be a joy and blessing to human hearts.

Christ has made every provision that His church shall be a transformed body, illumined with the Light of the world, possessing the glory of Emmanuel. It is His purpose that every Christian shall be surrounded with a spiritual atmosphere of light and peace. He desires that we shall reveal His own joy in our lives.

The indwelling of the Spirit will be shown by the outflowing of heavenly love. The divine fullness will flow through the consecrated human agent, to be given forth to others.

The Sun of Righteousness has "healing in His wings." Malachi 4:2. So from every true disciple is to be diffused an influence for life, courage, helpfulness, and true healing.

The religion of Christ means more than the forgiveness of sin; it means taking away our sins, and filling the vacuum with the graces of the Holy Spirit. It means divine illumination, rejoicing in God. It means a heart emptied of self, and blessed with the abiding presence of Christ. When Christ reigns in the soul, there is purity, freedom from sin. The glory, the fullness, the completeness of the gospel plan is fulfilled in the life. The acceptance of the Saviour brings a glow of perfect peace, perfect love, perfect assurance. The beauty and fragrance of the character of Christ revealed in the life testifies that God has indeed sent His Son into the world to be its Saviour.

The indwelling of the Spirit will be shown by the outflowing of heavenly love.

Christ does not bid His followers strive to shine. He says, *Let* your light shine. If you have received the grace of God, the light is in you. Remove the obstructions, and the Lord's glory will be revealed. The light will shine forth to penetrate and dispel the darkness. You cannot help shining within the range of your influence.

The revelation of His own glory in the form of humanity will bring heaven so near to men that the beauty adorning the inner temple will be seen in every soul in whom the Saviour dwells. Men will be captivated by the glory of an abiding Christ. And in currents of praise and thanksgiving from the many souls thus won to God, glory will flow back to the great Giver.

"Arise, shine; for thy light is come, and the glory of the Lord is risen upon thee." Isaiah 60:1. To those who go out to meet the Bridegroom is this message given. Christ is coming with power and great glory. He is coming with His own glory and with the glory of the Father. He is coming with all the holy angels with Him. While all the world is plunged in darkness, there will be light in every dwelling of the saints. They will catch the first light of His second appearing. The unsullied light will shine from His splendor, and Christ the Redeemer will be admired by all who have served Him. While the wicked flee from His presence, Christ's followers will rejoice. The patriarch Job, looking down to the time of Christ's second advent, said, "Whom I shall see for myself, and mine eyes shall behold, and not a stranger." Job 19:27, margin. To His faithful followers Christ has been a daily companion and familiar friend. They have lived in close contact, in constant communion with God. Upon them the glory of the Lord has risen. In them the light of the knowledge of the glory of God in the face of Jesus Christ has been reflected. Now they rejoice in the undimmed rays of the brightness and glory of the King in His majesty. They are prepared for the communion of heaven; for they have heaven in their hearts.

With uplifted heads, with the bright beams of the Sun of Righteousness shining upon them, with rejoicing that their redemption draweth nigh, they go forth to meet the Bridegroom, saying, "Lo, this is our God; we have waited for Him, and He will save us." Isaiah 25:9.

"And I heard as it were the voice of a great multitude, and as the voice of many waters, and as the voice of mighty thunderings, saying, Alleluia; for the Lord God omnipotent reigneth. Let us be glad and rejoice, and give honour to Him; for the marriage of the Lamb is come, and His wife hath made herself ready. . . . And he saith unto me, Write, Blessed are they which are called unto the marriage supper of the Lamb." "He is Lord of lords, and King of kings; and they that are with Him are called, and chosen, and faithful." Revelation 19:6-9; 17:14.